**Tirso's Art
in
*La venganza de Tamar***

Tirso's Art
in
La venganza de Tamar:

Tragedy of Sex and Violence

by

Everett W. Hesse

Spanish Literature Publishing Company
York, South Carolina
1991

Copyright 1991
Everett W. Hesse

Library of Congress Catalog Card Number 90-61991

ISBN 0-938972-17-0

Printed in the United States of America

Contents

Preface i
1. Images of Sexuality 1
2. The Four Elements 10
3. Deceit and Disillusion: Prologue 20
4. Deceit and Disillusion in *La venganza de Tamar* 26
5. The Subversion of Love 31
6. Tirso's Perception and Portrayal of a Rapist 43
7. Deconstructing *La venganza de Tamar* 50
Notes 57
Works Cited 61
Index to the Books Published by E. W. Hesse 65

Preface

The present opus commemorates my fiftieth year teaching and researching the *Comedia* (1941-91). It consists of a number of essays on Tirso's *La Venganza de Tamar* which I completed over the last several years without any idea at that time of including them in a monograph. Due to the backlog of essays awaiting publication in the several journals, I decided to gather my essays together in one place. A few have been published but have since been rewritten so as to make the present collection entirely new. Since all essays deal with the same play there is considerable duplication for which I beg the reader's indulgence. I have tried unsuccessfully to eliminate the repetition, but it has been impossible to accomplish it without damaging the unity of each chapter. The reader is therefore cautioned against reading all the chapters at one sitting and is urged to allow time to elapse between chapter readings.

My interest in *La venganza* began some time ago when I included it in seminars on the *comedia*. After repeated readings, reflexions and discussions with graduate students I realized that there was a tragedy of great distinction long neglected until A. K. G. Paterson's edition in 1969 made it available for more general use and use in classes and seminars.

The chapters analyze various elements of Tirso's art both poetic and dramatic. Each one constitutes an entity by itself independent of the other essays in the sense that one can start by reading the last chapter first, or in any order except chapters 3 and 4 which constitute a unit. My purpose in preparing this book is to show the depth of Tirso's ideas, his literary acumen, his skill as a dramatic poet and his humanity in this very poignant tragedy of the disintegration of a family.

Chapter One, "Images of Sexuality" shows how Tirso imparts meaning and substance to his tragedy by the large variety of images he employs to express the motivation and the emotions of his characters. The imagery is gustatory, appetitive, thermal, astrological, herpetological and theatrical; there are images relating to health, birds (of prey), fire, water, war, colors, gaming, weather, parts of the human body, flowers and at times in equivocal form. Tirso uses many images to represent one idea, or the same icon for the same idea. Often he joins two or more images in the same concept. This network of complex imaginal patterns also contributes to fleshing out the characterization.

Chapter Two takes up another aspect of Tirso's art: his ability to incorporate the four elements (air, fire, water, earth) of which the universe was supposedly composed, into his scheme of imagery. According to Cirlot, air and fire are active male, water and earth are passive and female. These four elements as a single entity or in conjunction with one another add another dimension to the play, infusing it with depth and substance. All of the elements express some aspect of the theme of erotic passion. They unify the action, intensify and deepen the characterization and produce an atmosphere of sensuality that permeates the entire work.

Chapter Three is prologue to Four; Three offers a background to the theme of deception by showing the extent of its appearance in drama all the way from new Greek comedy onward to the seventeenth century. Machiavelli's *The Prince* may have exerted some influence on sixteenth century Spanish drama, but the Spanish playwrights of the period were following the tradition of Roman comedy, widely performed in Renaissance Italy. The theme of deception occurs in Spanish drama of the seventeenth century comedies, tragedies, and in plays dealing with religion, the Bible, history, mythology, etc. The theme of deception is so widespread in the history of the theater that it raises a fundamental question about the human condition. Deceit, whether used as a theme or a dramatic device, can provide humor, pathos and tragedy; it can sharpen the conflict and advance the action. Without some form of deceit to produce a conflict, a play cannot long hold the attention of its audience.

Chapter Four extends the discussion of deceit and disillusion begun in the previous chapter to *La venganza*. All of the four main characters practice deceit and/or self-delusion. When events do not turn out according to expectation, disillusion occurs. Tamar out of sisterly love tries to help Amón regain his health but is disillusioned after being tricked into a charade and then raped. By his great love for his children David accedes to their every request and becomes bitterly disillusioned on discovering their delinquency. Absalón deceives his father with lies and false promises and suffers the greatest disillusion of all—death. Amón falls into self deceit, thinking that he can find happiness by compromising his sister's honor. His great disillusion also is death. Tirso raises some intriguing questions about the necessity for hope, and why some aspects of love at times may be an illusion that eventually becomes a disillusion.

Chapter Five underlines the subversion of love in *La venganza*. All four main characters love either themselves or their ideas. At first it seems that Tamar displays true sisterly love and concern for her brother's health. But, being human, she re(acts) imprudently by offering to be more of a "lover" in the "play" than the Ammonite princess was in real life, or in Amón's mind. Does Amón experience "love" for his sister which he attempts to justify in a sonnet (II, 1009-22), just prior to committing his dastardly act? David loves his children to the extent that he grants their every request without considering the consequences of his actions. Absalón swears his love for his father and Amón when in reality he hates both as they represent obstacles in his way to the throne. After Amón's death, Tamar shows her self-love by extolling her regained honor which now permits her to return to society unblemished. The play leaves unanswered the question: is hate a more powerful emotion than love?

Chapter Six introduces the reader to Tirso's keen analytical mind and his insight into the motives for rape and incest. Relying on Faculty Psychology, Tirso perceives Amón's sexual fixation as a product of the mind in its several functions: reason, imagination, memory and feelings.

Amón has never really loved any of his numerous girlfriends because no one measures up to his expectations regarding perfect physical beauty. He suffers a persecution complex, tormented by invisible enemies that exist in his mind as a result of his failure to confront reality. He lives in a world of fantasy, hoping that a woman with a sweet and charming voice will be beautiful. Discovering that he is in love with his own sister, he exploits her charitable nature and goodness of heart by luring her into an act of depravity that will end in tragedy for all.

Chapter Seven, "Deconstructing *La venganza*," raises the issue of the polysemic nature of signs. Unlike the New Criticism, Deconstruction does not accept the premise that a work of literature has a ready-made meaning, or one single meaning provided by the author to be ferreted out by the reader. The burden of fathoming the meaning is shifted to the reader who becomes a partner in creativity and who determines the meaning of the text.

Is the play just a question of rape and incest and how Amón will commit the crime with impunity? Or, is it as Paterson states, a play about justice? What concept of justice does Tirso present in the play? Is David fit to be king to administer justice when he ignores the threat to his life by Absalón, knowing full well the young man's ambition? Or, when he ignores Tamar as a victim and treats her as "basura"? Or, when he fails to admonish his son with a reprimand as part of the educational process? These and other hard questions will be examined in this chapter.

I am including an index to the books I have published from 1966 on to make more accessible to the reader the themes of the essays not always indicated by the book's title. All quotations are from the edition of Tirso's *La venganza de Tamar* by A. K. G. Paterson. Cambridge: Cambridge U P, 1969.

San Diego, CA *E. W. H.*

Chapter 1

Images of Sexuality

Very little has been written about *La venganza de Tamar* probably because the themes of incest and rape are somewhat delicate to the point of being almost taboo up to now. A. K. G. Paterson and Juan Valencia have broken fresh ground commenting on some of the symbols and images found in the play.[1] Paterson limits himself to the image of love as war and appetite; he does not devote a complete study exclusively to the other several images found in this tragedy. Valencia's article offers a brief but cohesive analysis of traditional symbols; he limits himself to flowers, food and colors. This chapter will attempt to present a more comprehensive and detailed analysis of the images already mentioned together with the other hitherto neglected in order to show their extensive dissemination and complexity. It will indicate how the images create an ambience of sexuality throughout the entire work, how they affect the characterization, point the direction of the action and how they call the reader's attention to the inevitable violence of rape/incest which leads to tragedy.

An image is a figure, representation or appearance of a thing usually introduced by means of language and created in the author's imagination.[2] When one thing is compared with another, metaphor is employed; it is a trope that consists of translating the basic sense of the words into figurative language. The imagination, which also creates symbols and concepts, belongs to two worlds—the psychological and the literary. In psychology the term "image" signifies a recollection of a passed experience; it is not necessary that it be visual. There are, for example, gustatory, culinary, thermal, and auditory images among others. They can represent a sensation or a perception. In the literary sense images reflect sensation or a feeling expressed in an esthetic form. Often Tirso mingles his imagery, placing two or more in the same metaphor for greater emotional impact. Some times he perceives an image in the form of a concept that unites art and philosophy. On other occasions he conceives images as symbols to externalize an inner reality with more clarity.

This chapter will be concerned with one aspect of sexuality, the rape of Tamar by her half-brother Amón and the violent acts that will offend the sensitive feelings of David and the members of his family. From the outset, Tirso prepares a climate of sexuality by subtle means whose object is to direct our attention to the sensuality of the play.[3]

Amón and his brothers Absalón and Adonías have just returned to Jerusalem during a truce which David has made with the Ammonites. The brothers have had a surfeit of war and seek recreation in the capital. Absalón suggests that they exchange their war tents for palace salons. In addition Absalón proposes they go courting. Here Tirso employs the ancient metaphor of the similarity between love and war as Paterson has mentioned (14). This similarity is present in both activities: a soldier scales the walls, a lover paces up and down the street where his girlfriend lives and eventually may ascend her balcony, "¿No asalta también paredes? / ¿Ventanas altas no escala? / . . . / Luego Amor a Marte iguala" (I, 72-6).

Amón is openly envious of Absalón's long hair. An abundance of hair on a man is a sexual image that attracts women. Amón makes fun of his brother who can sell locks of his hair to those women struggling to carry off some souvenir of the prince. Amón's servant Eliazer also ridicules Absalón's hair by means of a low joke, comparing it with a string of garlic, which turns the idea of beauty inside out. All Jerusalem calls him "socorre-calvas" (I, 104).

The brothers' conversation broaches the question of why Amón has not married one of his girlfriends. He has rejected all because no one measures up to his expectations of beauty. Tirso stresses the idea of sexuality when Absalón and Adonías propose to visit their father's concubines, an idea that scandalizes Amón. After the two have left, Amón decides to scale the walls and enter the seraglio garden in search of a woman.[4]

Tirso continues preparing slowly and subtly an atmosphere of love, this time in thermal imagery. Both Amón and Tamar feel the oppressiveness of the heat which warms their blood. The dramatist unites the images of the sultry weather with those of love. Tamar explains to her servant Dina why the latter does not feel love, "Porque no juntas las brasas / del tiempo al fuego de amor. / Mas, yo, que no puedo más, / y a mi amor junto el bochorno" (I, 296-9).

Then Tirso interlaces images of love with those of food, a phenomenon that stands out in almost the entire work. Dina comments that Tamar's mind is like an oven which can bake bread of tender thoughts for her lover Joab. Tamar agrees because she believes that Love thereby (re)pays its lovers with food.

Tamar and her servents are seated in the garden beside a spring among the flowers which resemble the "cojines de brocado" of her drawing room. Here Tirso plants flower imagery: flowers symbolize the brevity of life, the reality of death and they are a stimulus to enjoy life while it lasts. Beside the font, the women can slake their thirst, as if drinking from a golden chalice, a sexual vessel that later will contain poison.

The darkness of the night favors Amón's desire. It symbolizes the irrational and supports the concept of imprudence which Amón exhibits by invading the seraglio, placing his life at risk. Under the protection of the darkness Amón dares to approach a part of the wall where the spring is located to hear Tamar sing. The song deals with the loneliness the princess feels over the absence of her lover Joab. The happy bird that sings in the font will be the messenger who will bring news of her suffering to her lover and will gently reproach him of his neglect. The little bird symbolizes her longing and will be the courier of her amorous complaints. Amón is mesmerized by her sweet voice and falls in love with her without having first seen her, "O milagrosa fuerza / de un ciego dios que vence, / sin ojos y con alas / cuanto desnudo, fuerte" (I, 429-32).

Amón loses his balance and falls from the wall, which presages his imminent fall into sin. He is sure of not being discovered because the darkness of the night will conceal his identity. Moreover, he is disguised as a gardener. When Tamar out of compassion offers her hand to help him rise, Amón takes it and kisses it as a sign of gratitude and affection. But there is more. The hand is one of the parts of the body Tirso will exploit to intensify the idea of sexuality.[5] The sense of touch is the principal one of the five senses. To Amón the kiss tasted sweeter than honey. At the end of Act One, Amón exhibits his addiction to passion when he tells her, "que queráis o no queráis, / os he de besar la mano" (I, 832-3). This aggressiveness shows something of the character of the young man. It also suggests that the action will become more and more violent. On another occasion Amón will again force her to extend her hand so he can kiss it. Amón's life is literally in Tamar's hands because, if she fails to cook the food he wants, the prince will die.

Tamar indicates she will attend the nuptials of Josefo and Elisa, wearing a red gown. Amón already in his mind perceives her as "un clavel de grana" (I, 550). The color "red" symbolizes erotic passion in all its fire.[6] Red also represents the blood of the sex act both for Elisa as well as Tamar. Amón can think of nothing else except the red dress; it becomes a veritable obsession. The prince also dreams of the "encarnada aurora" which for him means "nueva vida." Tirso continues to unite the imagery of the red dress with the fire of sexual desire that burns in Amón's veins, thus underlining the volcano of passion that is about to erupt.

On discovering that he is in love with his own sister, Amón experiences more passion than ever after a brief period of anger and frustration. He compares himself with birds of prey like the falcon who cannot flee because its master has it blindfolded. Nor can Amón escape his master Love who has him trapped in his power, blind with passion. Like a bird of prey, Amón is about to swoop down on his victim, his own sister. He calls himself a monster of impossibilities. But appearances sometimes deceive and Amón becomes the victim of feminine enchantment, which he characterizes as "veneno en taza dorada, / sepulcro hermoso de fuera" (III, 2-3). The concept must be seen in two senses: as marauder and victim. When Tamar demands to know his identity, Amón describes himself as "una quimera encantada, / una esfinge con quien lucho / un volcán en nieve helada" (I, 814-16),[7] explaining the exteriorization of inner and contradictory forces which push him beyond the human power to control.

At the opening of Act Two when his friends offer him a fingerbowl, Amón rejects it paradoxically linking water with fire in his comment, "si con fuego me lavara, / pudiera ser que estuviera / mejor, pues me abrasa el agua" (II, 14-16). That is to say, one ought to cast water on the fire of love to extinguish it. But water thrown on fire can incite it more. Moreover, the images of fuego/agua by their contrariness can express a person's salvation or destruction.[8]

We now pass to the images expressing health. Tamar holds Amón's life in her hands because she can seek herbs and minerals to cure his illness. Amón knows this and begs her to take his pulse. He responds to Tamar's touch; her fingers serve as an instrument to understand the concept of the heart the prince is developing. He believes that it is impossible for her not to have diagnosed his illness correctly from his pulse. Amón invents another concept of the pulse: it is a tongue that speaks by signs. He continues with other concepts of his illness, explaining them in terms relating to their name: Tamar, *amar*; Amón, *amo*.

When Tamar asks how she can remedy his illness, Amón proposes a deception, "como es niño Amor se engaña / con cualquier casa fingida" (II, 671-2). Then he cites four examples of deceit to solve a problem. Turning to gustatory imagery, he applies it to his problem, "que sin que llegue al manjar, / le satisfaga la mesa" (II, 699-700). Amón suggests that Tamar play the role of his deceased Ammonite princess. Then she will be able to cure his mortal sickness. In theatrical concepts, Amón will write, direct and act in his own scenario—it will be a drama within a drama. During the performance Amón describes the various parts of Tamar's body with astrological imagery, "Zona soy que se corona / con los signos de oro bellos / de esos hermosos cabellos, / Estrellas son de esta zona / esos ojos; esas manos, / que al cristal envidia dan, / la vía láctea serán / de mis gustos soberanos" (II, 777-84).[9]

All this pretense which recalls to Amón the image of his ill-fated princess is now superimposed on Tamar's face. The latter is transformed into his pretended lover who consents to his courtship. Tamar will be an artificial spring to alleviate the patient's illness. During the course of the "drama" Amón feels better and schedules a tryst for later that evening in a scene full of feigned tenderness.

Joab, Tamar's lover, has overheard the scheme; he repeats her words mockingly and reproves her for an abominable love. By her conduct Tamar could destroy the marriage she expects. Not wishing to jeopardize her lover's honor nor her own, she reaches the conclusion that Amón must die.

When Amón feigns illness and goes to bed, Tirso again joins several images; those that express appetite, food, health and parts of the body. Amón begs his father to allow Tamar to cook and feed him. His diabolical scheme is obvious when he mentions that her eyes and hands will prolong his life because they fascinate him. Eliazer's song to mitigate Amón's melancholy reveals poetically the theme of love. The song of a beautiful young women who treads fields of flowers, dying of love and crying with laughter.

Tamar explains to Amón that she no longer is his pretended lover but Joab's wife. She will cook for Amón but against her will. He in turn reproves her for her fickleness (*mudanza*), comparing her in another metaphor with the ebb and flow of the tides, "crüel mudable Tamar, que en fin acabas en mar / por ser mar en la mudanza" (II, 974-76). The prince dismisses his servants and threatens to force Tamar's will. She comments that the food she is about to serve will not be seasoned because it is fictitious. That contrasts with the marriage of Josefo and Elisa, "fruto de un amor sazonado" (I, 743), a true love not feigned and mutually acceptable.

Tirso, the master craftsman, presents the marriage of Josefo and Elisa as a counterpoint to the illicit love of Amón and Tamar. But he leaves the theme of true love undeveloped so as not to divert the reader's attention from the main themes of rape/incest. Pallarés Navarro employs the words "love" and "passion" to distinguish " . . . entre el amor carnal y el amor sujeto a las convenciones de la moral social" (7). The difference is indiscernible by Amón at this point, "Tú sola has de ser manjar / del alma a quien avarienta / tanto ha que tienes hambrienta, / pudiéndola sustentar" (II, 1085-88). As Juan Valencia has observed, "Tamar es un 'bocado,' un manjar, que hay que saborear sólo con la violencia física . . . acto que . . . tal vez se confunda con la acción de comer" (3).

After the deflowering, Amón's erotic passion changes to hate. The prince feels repugnance and remorse, comparing her with the "fruta de Sodoma horrible, / en la médula carbón / si en la corteza apacible" (III, 13-15). The image is appropriate because the fruit of the Dead Sea were the apples of Sodom which, although in appearance attractive and savory, inside contained the ashes of the city, that is to say, its destruction (Paterson, 140, n. 13).

The images are loathesome and reflect his changed attitude toward Tamar. They evoke a feeling of repugnance when Amón compares her with the harpies, those voracious and monstruous birds of Greek mythology which, it was believed, could kill by their poison. He also compares her with the legendary basilisk which could kill by merely looking. The dramatist chooses his images judiciously. Harpies are a symbol of the usurpers of other people, possessive of those who maltreat others, and of prostitutes who fleece a man by taking his money

(Covarrubias, cited by Paterson, 140). Amón was deluded by external appearance which gave no indication of Tamar's character.

Having lost her most prized possession, her virginity, Tamar compares herself with a merchant without clients (III, 44-5) because "mujer gozada es basura" (III, 29). She reproves Amón, reviving gustatory images that he had employed previously. She figuratively throws them into his face, "lame el plato en que has comido" (III, 32), but this time with a hostile attitude. Next Tirso describes the rape in gambling terms. Tamar denounces Amón, "tahur de mi honor has sido, / ganado has por falso modo / joyas que en vano te pido" (III, 51-3). Having lost her virginity (which for her is life), she demands death as a recompense, Acaba el juego, traidor; / dame la muerte en barato" (III, 64-5). Tamar cannot repress a play on words, "... alza ... / la mano ... / y ganarás por la mano" (III, 73-5).

In a frenzy of rage, Amón verbally chastizes her with herpetological epithets, calling her, "sierpe ... / víbora ... " (III, 68, 81). Amón orders his servant Eliazer to expel her. The servant too makes use of gambling images, "carta Tamar viene a ser; / leyóla, y quiere rompella" (III, 84-5). Tamar complains to David about the outrage to her honor.

The princess connects several images to reinforce her sorrow. First she speaks of a "desatinado amor," and compares it with fire that leaves ashes as a reward. Then she speaks in images that suggest health and cleanliness. Ashes will be unable to remove the stain to her honor. Blood is the best cleansing agent. Amón's mortal illness was the plague of honor; moreover its contagion infected her.

Later Amón reminds David that the King himself had ordered Tamar to cook something savory to tempt the prince's jaded appetite. Tamar prepared some food but it failed to satisfy because Amón's hunger was in his soul. In her rage and sorrow Tamar thinks it would have been better to have cooked poison for him. Following the rape, Amón describes her as "veneno en taza dorada" (III, 2).

Later at Balhasor the gambling imagery is revived when Amón fails to recognize Tamar disguised as a shepherdess. He is fascinated by her eyes and describes them in gaming terms, "... fulleros / pues el alma me han ganado" (III, 860-1). Tamar responds in the same coin, "Cansaráos el juego presto, / y en ganando el primer resto / luego os querréis levantar" (III, 863-5).

Amón is again intrigued by her hands; he tries to take one but she refuses. Then Amón grabs one by force. What Tamar answers is repeated several times as an *estribillo*, "¡Qué amigo sois de forzar!" to underscore Amón's second attempt to violate her (III, 873, 885, 897). Alluding to her defilement, Tamar hands him a violet, " . . . [la] flor violada" (III, 893), symbol of her seduction. Tirso expresses in floral images Amón's proclivity to sexual violence. Tamar comments, "que a no perder yo una flor / no sintiera el mal que veo" (III, 884-5). After she reveals her identity, Amón calls her a basilisk again, " . . . tu vista me mató" (III, 903).

It is sheep-shearing time in Balhasor. One of the shepherds praises Tamar's beauty and inquires about the cause of her melancholy. He advises her to gaze upon her beauty reflected in the water. Another shepherd elaborates on the concept: washing in the water will remove the blemish to her honor.

But Tamar cannot remove the stain with water, only with blood. The shepherd advises her to cover the blemish with make-up. But this would be a falsification. Tamar knows that they are not *pecos* but *pecados*. Another shepherd asks her, "Es algún lunar acaso?" Tamar responds with astrological imagery, "No se muda cual la luna, / ni es la deshonra lunar" (III, 654, 656-7).

Absalón kills Amón in the banquet scene. Gustatory images reach a climax when Tamar, looking at Amón's lifeless body, condemns him, "Quédate, bárbaro, ingrato, / que en buen túmulo te han puesto. / Sepulcro del deshonesto / es la mesa, taza y plato" (III, 973-76).

To summarize. Tirso has availed himself of a long series of images to express the motivation and the emotions of his characters in *La venganza de Tamar*. At times he uses one image to represent love or erotic passion. Often he unites two or more images in the same concept. The imagery is gustatory, thermal, astrological, herpetological, and theatrical; there are images relating to health, birds (of prey), fire, water, war, colors, gaming, weather, parts of the human body, flowers and often in equivocal form.

The largest number of images are gustatory since Tirso has Amón associate the appetite of hunger with that of the biologic impulse. Before the defilement, the gustatory imagery is represented in a positive sense, but afterward in a negative sense to express remorse, frustration, rage, culpability and repugnance.

Tirso produces an ambience of sensuality to stress the illicit love between Amón and Tamar by his abundant use of sexual imagery throughout the work. He contrasts it with the true love of Josefo and Elisa. At first Tirso underlines the similarity of war and love. One must conquer the adversary by whatever means, by force, strategy, among others.

The images relating to fire are found in two senses: positive to signify love with its light and warmth, and negative to represent erotic passion and blood. In short, Tirso has created a *tour de force* with his imagery which gives substance to the text to the point of saturation, enriching it with poetry and drama. The images carry contrary ideas of beauty and ugliness which adorn the language, intensifying the violence and increasing the emotional effect on the reader. They express Amón and Tamar's emotions with great vitality and point the future course of the action. Tirso has left a beautiful example of his literary power to create an abundance of images around a central theme in its several aspects.

Chapter 2

The Four Elements

The symbols of sexuality discussed in the previous chapter are only one aspect of the totality of Tirso's imagery. In this chapter we will look at another phase: the four elements (air, water, fire, and earth) and what function they serve in Tirso's poetics and dramaturgy. The ancients believed that the four elements of which the universe is composed contain within themselves the necessities of life: air to breathe, water to drink, cleanse and cook, fire to warm and give light, and earth to produce food to sustain life. But at the same time they also possess the power to destroy life: water and the lack of air can suffocate and fire can burn to ashes. Paradoxically, they are at once a part of life and a part of death. Tirso possessed not only the vision to understand this phenomenon but also the ability, imagination and talent to dramatize the notion poetically and with feeling and force.

J. E. Cirlot regarded air and fire as active and male; water and earth passive and female. Some cosmogonies considered fire as the main element of all created things. The prevailing view is that air is the primary element. The compression or concentration of air creates heat or fire, the origin of all forms of life. Cirlot argues that air is related to three basic notions: 1) it created the breath of life and became speech; 2) in many mythologies air in the form of wind is associated with the idea of creation; and 3) it provides a space or environment for movement and for the egress of the life processes. Cirlot puts together light, flight, lightness, scent and smell, claiming they are all related to the symbolism of air. He also places in this category thoughts, feelings, memories and all aspects of climate and atmosphere.

Years ago Edward M. Wilson made one of the earliest studies of the four elements, selecting Calderón's plays as the basis of his essay. The present essay relies on Wilson only as a springboard for an excursus into an examination of the four elements in Tirso's *La venganza de Tamar*.

AIR

When one thinks of air one has in mind the invisible, odorless, tasteless gasses (nitrogen and oxygen) that surround the earth.[1] In *La venganza* air is used in many ways and for different purposes. Its main function is as a carrier in the sense of transport. One's reputation is extolled or denigrated as it passes from person to person by word of mouth. Speech fashions it and the air provides the means of its dispersion. King David's fame is well known to all, having been communicated by word of mouth. Amón compares himself with his father regarding their prowess as soldiers, "no soy tan soldado yo / cual dél la fama pregona" (I, 19-20). "Pregona" and "fama" are the key words whose meaning has been carried by air.

Birds occupy air space and their speed in flight is envied by man. Amón and his brothers are so eager to return home to Jerusalem from the wars that they describe their haste as "volando" like birds: one could say post haste, " . . . ¡Qué bien pensó / quien las postas inventó!" (I, 50-1).

Tamar, Amón's half-sister, sings "ligero pensamiento" and "Ay pensamiento mío" to her absent lover Joab hoping that a bird flying through the air will carry her message to him. Her servant Dina prognosticates what the wind can do if it is called upon, "tú al viento puedes llamar, / pues siendo tan celebrada / en la música Tamar / como en la belleza, a oírte / correrá el céfiro manso / alegre por divertirte" (I, 325-30). Hopefully the sound of her alluring voice whose fame has spread abroad over the air waves will reach Joab's ears, "¡Ay si mi amante me oyera!" (I, 350). Love is everywhere including the atmosphere, "no hay parte en que no entre Amor; / hasta aquí llegó su esfera" (I, 351-2). The atmosphere is the air of a locality or sphere and sphere is a place of influence.

Another aspect of air is the weather, i.e., the state of the atmosphere with respect to heat or cold, wetness or dryness, calm or storm, clearness or cloudiness. The hot humid weather described in the play evokes a negative reaction in several characters. Amón suffers unashamedly, "el tiempo está algo pesado" (I, 242), and "el calor que hace es cruel" (I, 267).

Combining the elements of air and fire, Tamar feels that her servant Dina endures the hot weather with less irritation, "porque no juntas las brasas / del tiempo al fuego de amor. / Mas yo que no puedo más / y a mi amor junto el bochorno" (I, 296-9). Tirso again mixes the elements of air and fire when Dina suggests to Tamar, " . . . serás un horno / en que a Joab cocerás / pan de tiernos pensamientos" (I, 301-3). That is, Tamar's mind, like an oven baking bread, will produce tender thoughts, which occupy air space, and which later will be transported by air to her lover's ear. The sultry weather has brought about a calm that is overpowering. Dina notes that "notable calma; no mueve / una hoja el viento siquiera" (I, 308-9). The lack of wind (an attribute of air) has created a lull that will evoke a different response in Amón and Tamar.

In another metaphor Tirso mingles air and water. In Tamar's garden a bird, a creature of air, drinking at the fountain, may be the carrier of her affection to her lover. The bird is addressed as a creature of the imagination,

> Ligero pensamiento
> de amor, pájaro alegre
> que viste la esperanza,
> de plumas y alas verdes,
> si fuente de tus gustos
> es mi querido ausente,
> donde amoroso asistes,
> . . . .
> pajarito que vas a la fuente,
> bebe y vente. (I, 353-9; 365-6)

The bird is a creature of air; its feathers and wings are green to symbolize the hope Tamar entertains for the bird's safe return with good news from her lover. Water in the fountain is a sign of the renovation of life which Tamar hopes to experience. Amón, who hears the song, is enchanted as the wind by its sweet sound, "a su melífluo canto / corrido el viento vuelve" (I, 385-6).

Thoughts and memories of past events lie in the air space of the mind. After Amón dismisses his visitors and servants who cannot cure his love sickness, he rails, "Morid todos, pues me matan / invisibles enemigos" (II, 222-3). The invisible enemies that haunt him represent the struggle between love and lust. He retains in his mind the image of his one-time love (the

Ammonite princess) and wishes it were not there, "si hubiera armas que mataran / la memoria que me aflige, / ¡qué buenas fueran las armas!" (II, 226-8). He needs desperately to inform Tamar of the nature of his illness. She encourages him to communicate by speech rather than by the guessing game of sign language, "si hablando no me lo enseñas, / mal tu enfermedad sabré" (II, 545-6).

In another complicated metaphor involving air and fire, Amón compares Tamar's beautiful eyes and hair with objects in the sky, "zona soy que se corona / con los signos de oro bellos / de esos hermosos cabellos. / Estrellas son de esa zona esos ojos; esas manos, / que al cristal envidia dan, / la vía láctea serán / de mis gustos soberanos. / Ay mis manos, que me abraso" (II, 777-85). The sun and stars follow their orbit in the sky, an open space. The stars and the sun, being composed of fire, emit heat and light.

The most poignant use of air occurs in the last scene of the third act when David hears the return of the prince on horseback. He goes to embrace the one he thinks is Amón (who has been killed by Absalón) and hugs only the air, "ay engaños lisonjeros / ¿Por qué con burlas pesadas / me hacéis abrazar los vientos?" (III 996-8). David wants only pity and lamentation to fill the air around him, "lástimas hable mi lengua; / no escuchen sino lamentos / mis oídos lastimosos" (III, 1061-3). Words designating speech, hearing, the human voice, the bird's song, and the space they occupy are the principal means Tirso employs in association with the element air.

WATER

The element water occurs frequently for several reasons. First, like the sacrament of baptism, it connotes newness of life. Secondly, some consider water the source of life. For example, in Botticelli's painting, Venus is born from the froth of the sea.[2] Water serves as a mirror in which women can see their beauty reflected. It is a cleansing agent to wash away any blemish except for the stain to one's honor. Water can signify human fickleness as represented by the ebb and flow of the tides. It can extinguish fire but a small amount can turn fire into a ranging inferno. Finally water symbolizes grief and lamentation in the form of tears. Water not only slakes one's thirst; it also refreshes the body when one bathes or sits by a stream in hot, sultry weather. Tamar sees the stream as giving life to those who sit on its shore and also the flowers that grow nearby (I, 310-14). In the garden Tamar sings a love song to her absent lover. It is addressed to a bird that quenches its thirst in the water. She implores the bird to visit her lover, convey her feelings of anxiety and return, "pajarito que vas a la fuente, / bebe y vente" (I, 365-6). In the second song these verses are repeated as an *estribillo* (I, 441-54). In the first song the bird is drinking at the fountain; in the second it will be drinking at a fountain near Joab. Tamar is jealous of the bird and compares her jealousy and the bird's projected sight of her lover with the inner vision she can only imagine, "celos estoy que goces / de mi adorado ausente / la vista, con que aplacas / la ardiente sed de verle" (I, 445-48).

Water functions as a mirror to reflect feminine beauty. We recall that David first saw Bathsheba bathing nude and fell in love with her. After he conveniently sent her husband away to die in combat, he married her, "hermosa Bersabé, ninfa del baño, / que sirviéndoos de espejo en fuentes frías" (II, 341-2).[3] Later, David sheds tears to show remorse for the death of Uriah, "dieron causa a un pequé, lágrimas mías" (II 344).

Both Salomón and David speak of tears, an element of water, in urging Amón to forget his melancholy and confide in his father, Salomón. Salomón: "No agüéis tan alegre día" (II, 453). David: "Aguado has el regocijo" (II, 473). Water in the form of tears is all David has left as he weeps over the loss of Amón, his first-born and heir to the throne. In a pitiful closing lamentation, David will shed tears of grief eternally, "tome eterna posesión / el llanto, porque sea eterno, / de mis infelices ojos / hasta que los deje ciegos" (III, 1057-60).

In the play within a play sequence, Amón persuades Tamar that everything feigned is an acceptable convention, that they are only playing the roles of lovers. Tamar will be the artificial spring that slakes his thirst, yet flows on by and will not let him drink (II, 714-6). Thus Amón thinks he will be restored to health, if only temporarily.

Seeing Tamar kiss Joab's hand, Amón becomes jealous and reproves her for being fickle by deserting him. He compares her with the changing of the tides, "crüel, mudable Tamar, / que en fin acabas en mar / por ser mar en la mudanza" (II, 974-6).

At Balhasor, a shepherd advises Tamar to look into a pool of water; then she can wash away the stain to her honor, "acá son espejos de agua, / que a los que mirarse van / muestran manchas y las quitan / en llegándose a lavar" (III, 638-41). The water can then perform the task of a purifying agent. But Tamar knows better. If water could eradicate her stain, she has already shed enough tears to have removed it (III, 642-5).

FIRE

The element of fire permeates the entire play. It has both constructive and destructive functions. In *La venganza* it often represents erotic passion, a force that both inspires and consumes. Under the sway of erotic passion, Amón feels a sense of exhilaration and excitement. Just before Tamar appears attired in a red gown, Amón in a soliloquy heralds the dawn of a new day, "salid ya encarnada aurora" (I, 647). He acts like a soul in torment, undecided over his forthcoming reaction to the sign of a "vestido carmesí" (I, 673), "dudo alegre, temo amando, / ay Amor, por qué de mudos / almas estáis abrasando" (I, 666-8). On seeing Tamar, he is consumed by a fiery passion, "ay Dios, ya el fuego me abrasa / de un vestido carmesí" (I, 672-3). It is almost as though he had developed a fixation for the color red, symbol of his flaming passion.

After Amón identifies Tamar as the object of his affection, he now longs to extinguish the flame of love, "más vale, cielos, que muera / dentro del pecho esta llama / sin que salga el fuego fuera" (I, 689-91). But once the spark of love has been struck, it is difficult to extinguish, especially since he himself is to blame for its renewal, "que yo mismo el fuego atizo / y brasas en que me quemo" (I, 807-8). Amón has temporarily suppressed his desire which he describes as "un volcán en nieve helada" (I, 816).

When the servants offer Amón a finger bowl to clean his hands, he expresses his feelings in a mixed image of fire and water, "si con fuego me lavara, / pudiera ser que estuviera / mejor, pues me abrasa el agua" (II, 14-16). After Tamar has consented to participate in the charade in which she will play the role of Amón's deceased lover, he is overjoyed. Whereas others have blood in their veins, he has fire.[4] Following the rape, Tamar pleads for justice before David. She explains that an unwanted love burns with fire at first but once burned out it leaves ashes as a remembrance (III, 192-9). Fearfully Amón enters his father's presence. He compares David's gray hair with cold ashes, vestiges of a fire that Love had once ignited (III, 338-41).

EARTH

The element of earth seems to imply origin and (re)generation. That has an obvious link with the Bible and myth in the story of creation. Genesis has two versions of the creation of man, in one of which "God created man in his own image" (Gen 1:27). Secondly, "God formed man of dust from the ground and breathed into his nostrils the breath of life, and man became a living being" (Gen 2:7). But before He created man and woman, God created the heavens and the earth. The "earth brought forth vegetation . . . plants . . . and trees" (Gen 1:12). The waters brought forth swarms of living creatures and the earth also yielded living creatures "according to their kind" (Gen 1:24).

Since Amón cannot find a woman who measures up to his expectations of physical beauty, his servant Eliazer suggests that he fashion "una dama de barro" (I, 140). The clay woman of perfect beauty that Amón seeks, he forges in his mind in accordance with his memory of the deceased Ammonite princess with whom he fell in love during a battle. The imagination like the earth functions as a medium of creation. In another sense the imagination like air is invisible but it occupies space in the brain where in the dark recesses of the unconscious it harbors intuitive knowledge.

The garden in which Tamar languishes and pines for her absent lover offers her a bed of flowers similar to the luxury of her drawing room in the palace, "en cojines de brocado, / sus flores de ciento en ciento / te ofrecen su real estrado / que, en fin, como eres Infanta / no te contentas con menos" (I, 315-19).

Seeking female companionship, Amón approaches the wall that surrounds David's seraglio.[5] Tamar's beautiful voice enchants him and suggests a connection with the story of Ulysses and the sirens.[6] His mind acts like a fecundating agent like the element earth. In fact Tamar herself may also be regarded as a creative force because she arouses the male to sexuality.[7] A shepherd foresees what will happen when Tamar treads the earth as a fecundating force, "Ya con vuesa hermosa vista / hierba el prado brotará / por más que la seque el sol, / pues vos sus campos pisáis" (III, 594-7).

The garden in which Tamar is singing to lessen the impact of the sultry weather may be viewed as a Garden of Eden.[8] Here Amón pictures in his mind Tamar along with David's concubines, "pisando el jardín florido" (I, 510). Learning that Tamar will wear " . . . vestido / carmesí" to a wedding tomorrow,

Amón compares her with a flower, "seréis un clavel de grana" (I, 549-50). Since Amón entered the garden he is a changed man, "libre de amor entré, ya salgo amante; / reíame antes de él, ya llorar puedo" (I, 557-8). Later after he discovers Tamar's identity, he curses the garden where he first met her, "mal haya el jardín, amén" (I, 679).

Upon his return to Jerusalem, David adorns his garb with bear's claws and lion's fur, "si después que los brazos guedejudos / del líbico león, fuerzas bizarras / hipérbole venciendo . . . " and " . . . galas haciendo las robustas garras / del oso informe . . . " (II, 293-5; 298-9). The adornments serve to commemorate his youthful conquest over these animals, creatures of earth, as a sign of his physical strength and military prowess and his domination of the earth.[9]

After the rape, Amón casts Tamar aside, hurling repulsive epithets at her, describing her in terms of the most loathesome creatures of the earth: a wild beast, a snake, a basilisk and a monster (III, 1-21; 68). By so doing, Amón diverts all sense of guilt from himself and attributes it to Tamar. This follows biblical tradition of blaming the woman for man's Fall (Gen 3:12).

At Balhasor the shepherds deck the houses with garlands of flowers, ivy and branches, fruits of the earth's bounty, in honor of their royal visitors, "y de flores, hierbas y ramos / entapicemos la casa" (III, 716-17). Cedar and palm branches decorate the doorways in honor of the return of a conquering hero (II, 249-67). Such was the recognition accorded David upon his return from the wars with the Ammonites. A victor's head was crowned with laurel and wine flowed freely in celebration (II, 296).

Laureta, a flower girl, hands a flower to each of the princes. The flowers she has chosen represent the character of each prince and the direction of his fate. She gives Amón an "azucena con una espadaña" and warns him of the significance of the lily with a pointed reed for his future. Since the pointed reed is shaped like a sword, she warns him, with a strong sexual significance, not to depetal a flower that has a sword to guard its honor (III, 782-93).

Adonías receives a larkspur ("espuela de caballero") with the admonition that a spur can do harm, and that he avoid courting a married woman (III, 803-5). Laureta presents a kingsray to Salomón ("corona de rey") for he is destined to be one of the greatest kings of Israel. She cautions him about making a mistake in his love life in old age (III, 811-17). Absalón is rewarded with a narcissus for having loved himself. His vanity has beclouded his judgment. Laureta urges him to trim his locks or they will raise him up on high, a comment he misinterprets (III, 821-33). Amón gets a violet ("flor violada") from Tamar whom he is about to rape again (III, 896-93).

Finally the shepherds adorn the houses with black poplar (which signifies sorrow), for Absalón marigold, and rose for Adonías, and the funeral cypress for Amón with its connotation of death.

In conclusion, Tirso emerges as a forerunner of the baroque style in that he presents metaphors containing the four elements which Calderón later develops into a complex stylization of forms. Tirso deploys the four elements so adroitly and unobtrusively that they blend neatly into his other images and thereby remain almost hidden from view. It is only upon a close reading that the treasure is discovered.

The element air serves many purposes. It is a carrier of speech and song to communicate information, frustration, and grief from one person to another. It transmits the reaction of some characters to the sultry, oppressive weather. It delivers a message of love that exists everywhere in the atmosphere. Air conveys thoughts and memories lodged in the spaces of the mind.

The element fire is mostly associated with Amón and underscores his uncontrollable, irrational and erotic passion which will lead him to death, the ashes of an extinguished fire. It has a similar connotation for David whose silvery gray hair represents to Amón the father's youthful escapades whose burning passion had already passed in the pre-stage action. Fire serves to stand for Tamar's beauty in heavenly terms. Only blood in its fiery red color can erase the stain to Tamar's honor.

The element water has many functions. It is a cleansing agent to wash away stain but not those to one's honor. It signifies renewal as it irrigates the fields and brings flowers, shrubs and trees to life. Like the ebb and the flow of the tides and a seascape in a storm, water can represent human fickleness and inconstancy. Water in the form of tears expresses grief and sorrow as when David mourns the loss of his eldest son.

The element earth plays a generative role. It nourishes fields and gardens, animals and humans. When Amón fails to find a woman who meets his expectations, he can fashion a statue of a beautiful woman of clay, a property of earth. The garden in *La venganza* is the place of *Conjunctio* where Amón falls in love with Tamar. Like earth Tamar is a fecundating agent, for wherever she treads flowers bloom and grass grows. The garden flowers stand for the sumptuous drawing room adorned with brocaded cushions. The flowers of earth given to each of the princes reveal their character and points to their ultimate fate. Attributes of the earth like palm branches, cedars and other woods adorn the farm houses to provide an air of festivity on the arrival of the distinguished visitors. Laurel dignifies the brow of the conquering hero. After the rape, Amón describes Tamar in terms of repugnant animals of the earth to deflect his own guilt in the crime.

    The four elements as a single entity or in conjunction with others add another dimension to the play, giving depth and substance to the action and overall meaning. They serve as the woof on which the dramatist weaves the threads of his figurative language. All of the elements express some aspect of the theme of erotic passion; they unify the action, intensify and deepen the characterization and produce a climate of sex and violence that permeates the entire play. Tirso follows no regularized pattern in his use of the four elements. He selects those elements appropriate to a given situation in order to create a more vigorous visual impression on the reader.

Chapter 3

Deceit and Disillusion: Prologue

The theme of deceit is very old.[1] It appears in Genesis where the serpent tempts Eve to eat of the fruit of the Tree of Knowledge. The serpent invites her to eat, "you will not die, for God knows that the day on which you eat of it your eyes will be opened, and you will be like gods, knowing good and evil" (Gen 3:4-5). Eve believes it and eats of the tree and seeing that it is good gives some to her husband who also eats of it of his own free will. Later, he blames the woman (Gen 3:12).

Deception as a dramatic motive continues and reappears in Greco-Roman comedy and passes on to Spain. New Greek comedy found a favorite formula that has lasted to this day: boy meets girl, an obstacle prevents their marriage, the obstacle is finally conquered by means of trickery and deceit, and the two are ultimately reunited.

It is possible that Machiavelli's *The Prince* (1513) influenced Spanish drama of the sixteenth century. In chapter xviii Machiavelli appears to support the idea that "the end justifies the means." He defines man as an egotistical animal dominated by an insatiable desire for material gain and motivated by self-interest. Men are easily deceived by appearances. Moreover, they are ungrateful, inconstant, liars and deceivers, covetous for their own benefit and faithful only when it is convenient. Machiavelli exhorts the prince to conceal this aspect of his nature and to be a consummate liar and an arch-hypocrite. He believes that men are somewhat naïve so that for the deceiving it is very easy to find some one who can be duped.

R. L. Grismer, on considering the influence of Plautus, Terrence and other dramatists of the sixteenth century Spanish theater, observes that Juan del Encina, Torres Naharro and other writers saw Roman comedy performed in Italy. According to Grismer, modern European drama originated in Ferrara with the translation of Plautus' *The Menaechmi* into Italian about 1486(10). O. Arróniz has also noted the Italian influence on Spanish drama and the diffusion of the theme of deception.

Examining Lope de Rueda's *Los engañados*, J. P. W. Crawford gives first place to the theme of love, arguing that deception arises from appearances. In this play there are two sets of twins of extraordinary similarity whose disguise and changes of name complicate the plot. The argument is complex and treats of the theme of love in the context of deceit and self-deceit. In reality there would be no play if there were no deception because one theme depends on the other and produces tension and conflict.

Jean Canavaggio in an edition of Cervantes' *entremeses* has noted the extensive use of deception in *El retablo de las maravillas*, *La cueva de Salamanca* and *El viejo celoso*, "entre los motivos así dramatizados se destacan en seguida los ardides y embustes de la mujer taimada o meramente lista" (18).

El retablo de las maravillas deals with a sly deception carried out by the impresario, Chanfalla, who knows how to deceive the public. No one of Jewish blood or of illegitimate parents—says Chanfalla—can see what is happening on stage. Since no one will admit to descent from a questionable lineage, everybody swears falsely to have seen the wonders of the *retablo*. Cervantes points out how easily one can deceive people by means of their own imagination and a false sense of pride.

The tradition of deception appears in burlesque form in the Renaissance theater. Juan de la Cueva's *El infamador* is perhaps the best example of the theme, and anticipates the character of D. Juan in *El burlador de Sevilla*, a seducer of women. As I have noted elsewhere, D. Juan not only mocks women but men also. Norman O. Brown has expounded the theory that the deceiver (*burlador*) was a well-known figure among people of antiquity and their mythology (10-11). Karl Kerényi calls Hermes a "master thief" especially in the art of sexual love (28).

Alfredo Hermenegildo has found deception in sixteenth century Spanish tragedy. He observes that in Virués' most outstanding work *La gran Semíramis*, " . . . uno de los rasgos más característicos . . . es la mentira" (498). He comments that "el engaño parece con más frecuencia y sobre todo como elemento de gran eficacia dramática" (499). Another authority, H. J. Chaytor, in his edition of the *Arte nuevo* underlines nothing specific in his preface about what Lope had written, but "el monstruo de la naturleza" knew very well that deceiving with the truth was what pleased the public more (325-8). We will now examine the art of deception in some of the best known plays of Lope, Tirso and Calderón, in comedies, tragedies, biblical and religious plays. We shall focus our attention only on those aspects of deception that stand out in each play.

Lope's *La dama boba* is a delightful comedy of love and deception. Two sisters are in love with the same man, Laurencio. Nise is an intellectual; Finea is dull-witted. Laurencio prefers Finea and by subtle and comic means he teaches her about love. Later he has to teach her how to be dull-witted. Finea comments, "mil gracias, Amor, te doy, / pues me ensenaste tan bien, / que dicen cuantos me ven / que tan diferente soy" (III, 2060-63). According to Finea, women have a natural inclination to deceive because even before they were born, they deceived. While still in the mother's womb, they gave their parents to understand that they were able to mock their desires.

The action of *El perro del hortelano* turns on deceit; a deception will help resolve Diana's problem. She is the countess of Belflor and in love with her secretary Teodoro whom she cannot marry because of the inequality of their social ranks. Teodoro's servant Tristan asserts that his master is old Ludovico's long lost son. The deceit is not done with malice. The audience approves of the deception because it gives Ludovico the hope of seeing his lost son. Full of joy, the old man is convinced that Teodoro is his son because of the similarity of facial features. Thus we see that the success of the deception and the self-deception indicates that the difference in social rank will not impede a marriage when love exists. Teodoro confesses the deceit to Diana, but it does not matter to her, "que el gusto no no está en la grandeza, / sino en ejecutarse el alma / aquello que se desea" (III, 950-52).

Deceit has just an important a role in tragedy as it does in comedy. *El castigo sin venganza* is a powerful love tragedy of hate, treachery, adultery and vengeance. It treats of the fateful marriage of the Duke of Ferrara and Casandra. Federico, the Duke's illegitimate son, falls in love with his stepmother. Since the Duke has broken his marriage vows by visiting prostitutes, Casandra decides to take vengeance, allowing Federico to court her during the Duke's absence. Upon his return, the lovers fear that their love will be discovered. On being informed of Federico's treachery, the Duke plans a punishment which will not be taken for revenge. He orders Federico to kill a traitor, an enemy of the dukedom. Federico kills Casandra, unaware that the "traitor" is in reality Casandra. Then the Duke falsely accuses his son of murdering his stepmother because she was pregnant with the future heir of the duchy.

One of the more striking recourses used to accentuate the deceit in *El castigo* is irony. The audience is in on the ruse and enjoys seeing a character duped. When the Duke asks Batín how Casandra and Federico got along, his servant responds with a part of the truth which Lope called "engañar con la verdad"—to lie by omission, since the Duke does not lie directly and his deception consists of concealing a part of the truth.

Deceit is found in many *comedias* to evoke risibility by means of jokes and tricks by the *gracioso* (clown). But what is of greater importance is the serious aspect of a deception. Fabia, the superannuated go-between in *El caballero de Olmedo*, awakens Inés's curiosity by the articles for sale that she carries in a basket. She has slyly placed a letter from Alonso among the articles. She comments astutely, " . . . Diste con él / cual si fuera para ti" (I, 363-70). Fabia's trick is done with malice; she expects to collect money from a deceitful act, but the two lovers are already in love and do not need the services of a third party. Nevertheless, Alonso deceives Inés when he informs her that he must return home so that his parents may know that he has emerged unharmed from the bullfight. He deceives her without malice. He had promised to marry her but apparently he has changed his mind.

To play a role forms an integral part of deceit and occurs frequently in the *comedia* when a character attempts to surmount obstacles which impede the realization of his will. The classic example is perhaps *Don Gil de las calzas verdes*. Disguised as a man, Juana pursues her faithless lover, D. Martín, to Madrid. There she deceives everybody including her recently hired servant Caramanchel. Her other servant Quintana calls her a "retrato de engaño" to which Juana responds, "y mi remedio seré" (II, 1122-23). Tirso is a master of deceit; *Don Gil* is full of disguises, lies, tricks, changes of identity and role-playing. With these and other deceptions, Juana succeeds in conquering Martín and making him fulfil his promise of marriage. The timing continues at a more rapid pace with each new deception, creating suspense because judgment could turn the comedy into a tragedy. Since she is a consummate actress, Juana knows how to change her identity rapidly thus avoiding a catastrophe.

In addition to lies and deceits, we now turn to another type of deception, one which is astonishing: that of representing God as a participant in a deception. In the unfolding of *El burlador de Sevilla*, D. Gonzalo falsely encourages D. Juan, " . . . Dame esa mano, / no temas; la mano dame" (2749-51). Here D. Juan's conscience begins to prick him and he explains to D. Gonzalo, "a tu hija no ofendí / que vio mis engaños antes" (2767-68). Not wishing to show fear, D. Juan offers his hand. In that moment flames engulf him. If D. Gonzalo is God's representative on earth, does God's justice deceive like that of a mortal? Archimede Marni justifies the double sense of D. Gonzalo's ethical values as an example of counterpassion.

In Calderón's *El médico de su honra*, during the absence of Prince Enrique, Mencía's father marries his daughter to one Gutierre who is represented as the epitome of an extremely jealous husband. On returning, Enrique is stunned to learn of Mencía's marriage. One day Enrique visits her to hear her explanation when Gutierre returns home unexpectedly. To protect their honor, Mencía hides Enrique. By a ruse, she expels him from the house, feigning that the intruder may have been a thief. Gutierre searches the house and comes across the Prince's dagger with his insignia. His imagination runs wild and he suspects Mencía has been unfaithful. One night when Gutierre returns home secretly, he finds his wife asleep in the garden. He extinguishes the light and she awakens. In his imagination he wonders why no servant attends her. He decides to change the timbre of his voice, speaking quietly and imitating the prince. Then he deceives Mencía, creating a false reality for her.

Rosaura pretends to be a man in Act One of *La vida es sueño* and in Act Two she plays the role of Astrea, lady-in-waiting to Princess Estrella, in order to deceive her faithless lover. Astolfo recognizes Rosaura in spite of her disguise. He asks her to abandon the deception, but she refuses, preferring to take vengeance. Rosaura struggles with Astolfo to recover her picture. When Estrella appears, Astrea (Rosaura) deceives her with a partial truth in recounting the struggle for her portrait.

Deceit is also found in Calderón's religious play *El mágico prodigioso*. Lelio, who had been enamored of Justina, accuses her of deceit when he sees the figure of a man emerge from her balcony. She accuses him of building castles in the air. Angrily, Lelio dashes out of the room, shouting, "si es engaño o no es engaño, / así veré el desengaño" (II, 1610).

Deceit and Disillusion: Prologue

Deception is one of the most widely diffused themes of the *comedia*. It appears in all classifications: comedies, tragedies, and plays dealing with religion, the bible, history, etc. It can be the principal or subordinate theme. Often it is a means of increasing dramatic tension. It can also be a technique to provoke laughter. It has a serious aspect even in comedy where deception takes various forms: lies, tricks, jokes and the playing of a role thus creating a play within a play. It can be executed with benevolent or malevolent intent. In both cases it is carried out for personal interest. It can produce comedy or tragedy. Frequently deception is tied to other themes like love, jealousy, egoism, the lack of communication, ambition, power, treason, parody, etc. It is not limited to one sex or any one class in society.

Deception advances the plot. It also complicates it by means of lies thus putting the resolution in doubt. It serves as an instrument whereby characters of greater imagination can manipulate others endowed with lesser imagination. In some plays the hero is blind with passion and needs the assistance of a servant to speak for him and map out a course of action.

The dramatists of the period on accepting the dual proposition of theater as "deleitar aprovechando," leave us with the tantalizing question that Machiavelli had asked, is deceit a part of the human condition? It may have entered the minds of seventeenth century Spanish playwrights who left an indelible impression of it in their dramas.

Chapter 4

Deceit and Disillusion in *La venganza de Tamar*

We will now examine in detail the theme of deceit in *La venganza de Tamar* and the subsequent disillusion which occurs when the expected turns out to the contrary causing frustration, cynicism, anger and the desire for revenge. We shall limit our discussion to the four principal characters: King David, and his offspring, Amón, Absalón and Tamar. The other relatives appear in only minor roles in the work. Amón's rape of Tamar constitutes the main action; Absalón's ambition to rule comprises the secondary action. There are several links which bind the two actions: one is Amón, an obstacle to Absalón's ascent of the throne; another is the present occupant of the throne, David, whom Absalón would not hesitate to assassinate in order to gain the throne. Tamar appears in both actions and once dishonored, she provides Absalón with a pretext to kill Amón, especially after David pardons him for the crime of rape.

Deceit and disillusion are not only themes in *La venganza* but also techniques that sharpen the conflict and at the same time advance the action. In addition, they serve a philosophic purpose by showing the disintegration of love in all its aspects when one of the parties allows his passions to overcome good judgment in human relationships.[1] We begin with Amóns's incestuous love for his half-sister Tamar, followed by sisterly love, Absalón's narcissistic love and his desire to rule, and finally David's blind love for his children.

AMÓN

Tormented by the memory of an impossible love for an Ammonite princess now deceased, Amón falls into a spell of melancholy and withdraws from society. Confiding in Tamar as a last resort, he relates his impossible love to her. His memory preserves the image of a deceased princess which he now projects on to Tamar, "mi princesa mal lograda / fue imagen de tu hermosura; / suspender mi mal procura, / en su nombre transformada" (II, 701-4).

Amón proposes a charade, a drama within a drama. Tamar will play the role of the princess, and Amón that of her lover. To convince Tamar of the drama's unreality, Amón recounts four analogues to demonstrate that Cupid (Love/Amor), being a child, can be deceived by any pretended thing (II, 671-2).[2] Because of their blood relationship, Amón promises that there will be no duplicity, "serás fuente artificial, / que alivia al enfermo el mal, / sin beber mientras que corre" (II, 714-16). Amón deceives her with a ruse. The "date" will continue until Amón transgresses the law concerning brother/sister relationship. Amón plays his role seriously but Tamar takes the episode for a "donosa aventura."

After the "rehearsal," Joab, who has seen and heard the charade from ambush, reproves Tamar for her infidelity, pointing out that she compromised and tarnished her own honor as well as that of her fiancé. Tamar is disillusioned, believing that she was helping Amón regain his health. Finally, Tamar is convinced by Joab's advice and kisses his hand in gratitude. Observing the episode from ambush, Amón, misinterpreting her motives, is greatly disillusioned by Tamar's "treachery."

Having recourse to deceit, Amón decides to carry out Jonadab's scheme to seduce the imprudent Tamar. It will be another deception in which Tamar is to prepare Amón's food. After the defilement, Amón is disenchanted again. In his frustration and anger he reprimands her; she in turn scolds him for having caused her dishonor. Her good intention to restore Amón to health has failed.

Later, approaching the King, Amón addresses his father in loving terms, "amoroso padre," and "piadoso padre" (III, 362; 367). On receiving David's pardon, Amón is overwhelmed by such a manifestation of love and promises " . . . no ofendelle desde hoy" (III, 393).

In Balhasor Amón is fascinated by the beauty of a shepherdess, Tamar disguised. He seizes her hand by force and excuses himself, "pues su hermosura me esfuerza" (III, 871). Tamar discloses her identity and comments, "¡qué amigo sois de forzar!" (III, 873; 897). Amón is disillusioned by the discovery of her identity, "¡no esperaba, cielos, yo / tal principio de comida!" (III, 904-5). Amón has failed to find happiness, only disilusion in his idea of love.

TAMAR

Tamar's compassion for Amón in his state of melancholy knows no limits, "hierbas y piedras buscara, / experiencias aprendiera, / montes ásperos subiera, / filósofos consultara" (II, 497-500). After hearing Amón's story about the Ammonite princess, Tamar feels even a deeper compassion for her brother, "me aflige más tu querella" (II, 664). Therefore, she willingly agrees to participate as his lover in the charade. In fact, she offers to perform the part in such a manner, "que en mí tu dama hallarás, / quizá más correspondiente / que la que ansí te abrasó" (II, 720-2). After eavesdropping on the "rehearsal," Joab has difficulty distinguishing between "hermanada afición" and "hermanos carnales" (II, 834; 836). She denies any evil intention. She is so disenchanted that she desires Amón's death. Later, she informs Amón that she no longer wants "palabras disfrazadas" and "engaños" and that she will seek an "honesto amor" with Joab (II, 963-965).

After the deflowering, Tamar thinks of her self and her future, realizing that, "mujer gozada es basura," and "¿Dónde iré sin honra, ingrato?" (III, 29; 42). Failing to receive justice at David's hands, she would prefer to live among wild beasts where her honor would be secure (III, 314-17).

In Balhasor some shepherds advise her to adopt a façade of "postiza virginidad" (III, 649). They suggest she cover the stain "con solimán" (III, 651). But the stain can only be eradicated with blood. Once a woman has lost her honor in seventeenth century Spanish society, she becomes a pariah.

After Absalón slays Amón, Tamar emerges triumphant with the thought that vengeance has conquered love, "ya podré mirar la gente / resucitando mi honor, / que la sangre del traidor / es blasón del inocente" (III, 969-72).

ABSALÓN

Narcissistic love is reflected not only in Absalón's pride and his vanity but also in his ambition to rule. He would even kill his own father to ascend the throne. David overhears the threatening words and confronts Absalón with them. The latter escapes from the predicament, deceiving his father with a blatant lie.

At first David does not permit Absalón to take Amón to their country estate at Balhasor. Absalón wishes to test his father's love. When the King relents, Absalón responds, "cierto ya de tu amor quedo" (III, 550). Absalón lies regarding his love for Amón, commenting slyly, " . . . no le ama más / que yo nadie en Israel" (III, 478-9). His strategy is to slay Amón in Balhasor to carry out Tamar's vengeance. The love he professed for his father and brother is a façade behind which he conceals his true motives: his passion to rule and his gaining the throne. A witch predicts that if Absalón allows his beautiful locks to grow any longer, he will soon find himself, "en alto por los cabellos" (III, 833). Absalón misinterprets the prophecy and dies hanging by his hair from the branches of a tree.

DAVID

David suffers an overwhelming disillusion after discovering that his children have deceived him with flattery, lies and false promises. On returning to Jerusalem, he finds his favorite son Amón in a state of melancholy. When Amón refuses to speak to him, David's frustration and anger are reflected in his question, "¿pero qué contento iguala / al dolor que causa un hijo? (II, 475-6). The King begs him to show some sign of affection, "¿que no mereciera yo, / aunque fingiéndolo fuera, / una palabra siquiera / de amor?" (II, 477-80). David's disillusion reaches a climax when he can no longer communicate with his son, "¿Qué vale el reino que gano, / hijos, si al Príncipe pierdo?" (II, 487-8).

Without really thinking about the import of Amón's seemingly modest request, he orders Tamar to prepare a meal for her brother. David is again disillusioned on learning of Tamar's violation. Because of his great love for Amón, he never expected to be dishonored by such outrageous behavior. Recalling his past sins which God has forgiven, David decides to pardon Amón (III, 374-7).[3] Trusting in Absalón's love for Amón, he allows the latter to leave for Balhasor, but with misgivings.

Toward the end of the play, David anxiously awaits the return of his offspring. In his imagination he "sees" the figure of Amón, his beloved, his favorite son. He longs to embrace and kiss him. The stage direction reads, "Va a abrazar el viento" (III, between vv 993-4). David is disillusioned by the " . . . engaños lisonjeros: / ¿Por qué con burlas pesadas / me hacéis abrazar los vientos?" (III, 996-8). He conjectures that Absalón has killed Amón. Absalón's promises were false. The daughter defiled, Amón dead and Absalón a liar, David can stand it no longer. What disillusion a father must suffer for his children's behavior. His affliction recalls another verse full of bitterness, frustration and anger, "¿Esto es, cielos, tener hijos?" (III, 284).

To conclude: deceit and disillusion are scattered throughout the entire work and affect the lives of Amón, Tamar and David. Absalón with his dream of ruling will not live to suffer a disillusion of his abominable plan to kill his father and Amón in order to ascend the throne. Perhaps his death is his greatest and only disillusion. Amón suffers under the illusion that he will be able to find happiness by means of his love affair with Tamar. When she withdraws from the charade leaving Amón alone, he is disillusioned over the failure of his plan.

For the sake of her brother's health and out of her love, Tamar attempts to help him, even to participating in a charade, an admitted deception. When her fiancé Joab catches her in the role of an inamorata, Tamar realizes that she has deceived herself in doing good.

David, who never expected his children to become delinquents, experiences a bitter disillusion on recognizing that all his love and sacrifice for his children have been in vain. He is a pitiable figure who begs Amón for even a pretended sign of love.

Tirso seems to be saying that deceit is necessary for hope, and a disillusion occurs when hopes are not realized. He also seems to be saying that all love founded on illusion is a self-delusion because it is unreal and does not bring happiness. The most disheartening event occurs when one helps another and it ends in a disillusion because the other has stooped to a deception. The play, or rather the tragedy, shows the triumph of hate and the failure of love.

Chapter 5

The Subversion of Love in Tirso's *La venganza de Tamar*

I

Love in the majority of romantic works of literature conquers all ("amor omnia vincit"), but in Tirso's poignant tragedy *La venganza de Tamar*, it is defeated and hate triumphs accompanied by cruelty, selfishness, dishonor, violence and revenge. Love connotes tenderness in a relationship, mutual respect, trust, fidelity, caring, sharing and commitment. Such a code of ethics repudiates selfishness, cruelty and an obsession with sex that enslaves its possessor who subverts love converting it into lust. In *La venganza* it is not only the romantic love that is overturned but also love in other aspects: paternal, family, and brotherly/sisterly.

Romantic love succeeds only in the marriage of Josefo and Elisa, which Tirso plays in low key to avoid distracting the reader's attention from the disenchantment of love in the main action. It serves as a contrast to the lust in Amón's feeling toward Tamar. It is an "amor no sazonado" contrasted with an "amor sazonado" between Josefo and Elisa. Centuries ago Heraclitus discovered the phenomenon of the sudden reversal of contrary emotions as from love to hate, which he called "enantiodromia."

The present chapter will examine the subversion of love as Tirso artfully and dramatically depicts it in *La venganza*. It will seek out the causes of the subversion of love and underscore Tirso's knowledge and understanding of the feelings and emotions in his portrayal of human behavior. Finally, it will reveal Tirso's ability to explore the workings of the human mind as it functions in imagination, thinking, reasoning, memory, recall and feeling in its relation to love. Modern psychologists consider the brain as the primary sex organ in the body. The brain receives stimuli from the senses which in turn are relayed to the brain. The brain then sends out responses to the senses in the form of sexual arousel by which the human entity seeks to possess what it has perceived as beautiful. An adage says that beauty is in the eye of the beholder; that is in the mind's eye, or what the eye has perceived as it is transmitted to the mind which reacts accordingly. The essay will explore the theme of subversion as it appears in all of the four leading characters, Amón, Tamar, Absalón and David. All quotations are from the text by A. K. G. Paterson and refer to act and verse number.[1]

II

Amón, David's eldest son and heir to the throne, is portrayed as incapable of love. From the opening of the play the reader notes that Amón is "singular" (I, 42), he hates war and his brother Adonías states the rest of the problem plainly, "nunca fuiste enamorado" (I, 83). Another brother, Absalón, has reached the same conclusion (I, 152). Tirso paints Amón as a playboy who has many female friends but no one that he considers attractive enough to marry; all are marred by flaws. He has picked up Absalón's idea of perfect beauty but unfortunately, he seeks it in an imperfect world. There is a hint of his aversion to marriage when he pities the married man "con una mujer a cuestas" (I, 161). His mind recalls the image of the Ammonite princess which he cannot dislodge. The more he thinks about her, the more obsessed he becomes with sex. For Amón she was beautiful, beauty personified and beauty that was lacking in his previous girlfriends. Amón's obsession with love primarily as lust (or sex) simmers in his mind as he thinks of David's many concubines languishing in the seraglio, waiting for young lovers.

Not only is Amón averse to marriage but there is a strong suggestion that he is also prejudicial against women whom he considers a "frágil sujeto" and "un animal imperfecto" (I, 226-7). Another inkling of his bias toward women occurs when he wishes women were not necessary for purposes of procreation (II, 33-7).[2]

Amón is envious of Absalón's physical beauty and his conversational ability which help to make him more attractive to women (I, 85-6). Amón is headstrong and wishes to do as he pleases (I, 275; 287-90). He has always been his father's favorite son. David indulges the son's every whim as when he orders Tamar to cook for and feed her half-brother.

After hearing Tamar's singing, Amón concludes that any woman with such a sweet voice must be beautiful (I, 411-13); at this point he is unaware of Tamar's identity.[3] He hopes that fate has given her a beautiful face to match her singing, but he has some misgivings, "aunque no se suele hallar / con buena voz la hermosura" (I, 497-8).

Learning of Tamar's decision to attend the wedding of Josefo and Elisa attired in a red dress, Amón can think of nothing else. He wishes to be alone with his obsession, "no quiero conversación, / porque ya con quien me entiendo / sola es mi imaginación" (I, 626-8). He turns inward, and without having seen her face, he is enamored of her. He is again assaulted by contradictory ideas and questions that indicate his fear of losing her. Suppose she chooses to wear a gown of another color. How will he recognize her? What if she decides not to attend? When he finally discovers her identity, he realizes it is an impossible love since he has fallen in love with his half-sister. He cannot decide whether to continue courting her or to forget her. This indecision elicits a response that describes his inner state, "un compuesto de contrarios" (I, 810), besieged by "invisibles enemigos" (II, 223). Tirso dwells on this inner struggle, describing the princess's soul as "de contradicciones hecha, / de imposibles sustentada" (II, 235-6) in order to stress more vividly the deterioration of love in this awesome tragedy.

Previously Amón had become enamored of a beautiful Ammonite princess, that is, he fell in love with her beauty, not the princess as a person as he had only seen her beauty from a distance. It was an attachment nurtured by his imagination which perceived her as the epitome of beauty. Once having beheld the beauty of the princess, whom he had actually never met, he then compares her with all his other girl friends who are all lacking in perfect physical beauty. His imagination now conjures up an ancient concept that beauty in any of its manifestations attracts just as the Siren's singing lured sailors to their destruction. Amón's image of ideal beauty and his quest for it in rejecting his former inamorata, leaves others to question his capacity to love (I, 31-44; 81-3).

Amón tries to deny reality vowing never to love (I, 143); he wants compassion, an attribute of love, for his "mala condición" (I, 144). This is how his imagination forges reality for him. When he hears Tamar sing, he enters more deeply into his world of fantasy and his imagination queries, "¿Quién duda que es hermosa? / ¿Quién duda que conviene / su cara con su canto?" (I, 411-13). He jumps to a false conclusion based on pure speculation, thus creating for himself an "imagined reality" by wishful thinking. Like a typical galán in a *comedia*, Amón experiences pangs of jealousy without even having seen the girl of his dreams.

Amón is disturbed by the possibility that her face may not be as beautiful as her voice. The common idea was that a fair voice seldom finds a fair face (I, 494-8). Although living in a world of fantasy, here and there Amón begins to imagine that she may not measure up to his expectations. Other instances of this likelihood are found as for example, "Como a la voz iguale / la belleza, que suele / ser ángel en acentos / y en rostro ser serpiente" (I, 397-400). Amón's sonnet lays bare his feelings of uncertainty that produces mental problems which he cannot solve (I, 555-68). This unsureness is disconcerting and is one of the factors of his divided self. Knowing that Tamar is to wear a red gown to the palace for the wedding of Josefo and Elisa, he is assaulted by more doubts. Will she appear in a red dress or in one of another color? Will she come at all? Tirso expresses this tension of intense passion in contrasting terms, "Dudo alegre, temo amando" (I, 666).

On discovering that the object of his affection is Tamar, his half-sister, Amón momentarily appears frustrated and is willing to abandon his erotic pursuit. But the power of love forces him to continue courting her.

His love or passion for the deceased Ammonite princess is now transferred to Tamar. He creates a "reality" for himself and Tamar by suggesting a way to satisfy his yearning without compromising her. Asking for pity, Amón devises a charade in which they are to enact the role of lovers. He offers four analogues to assure her that love can be deceived (II, 673-88). Tamar is convinced and agrees to play her role fully (II, 720-8). The sensuality of Amón's love is reflected in the tactile sense when he seizes her hands and kisses them using mouth and lips, "pagando en besos agravios / quien se hiciera todo labios / para gloria de esta boca (II, 518-20).

Tirso provides what he perceives as the necessary details that will enable the reader to better understand the ramifications of Amón's "love." Amón is ashamed to speak about it even to

Tamar at first, fear of ridicule and rejection being the essential ingredients. He experiences love as cruel, punishing him with torment and fire in his veins (II, 515-16, 524). It is also deceptive and cannot be trusted (II, 527). At first he does not speak openly of his impossible love for the deceased princess. He communicates in signs. The pulse is a tongue that speaks in signs. Moreover, their names suggest love: T(amar) and Amó(n). His memory preserves the image of the deceased princess which he now projects on to Tamar, "Mi princesa mal lograda; / fue imagen de tu hermosura; / suspender mi mal procura, / en su nombre transformada (II, 701-4).

Amón prepares the love scenario in his mind. Tamar is to pretend to be the Ammonite princess. Amón, her lover, will visit her at a rendezvous that evening. He will enter through a secret doorway in the wall and she will come down to meet him. Having talked over the scenario like members of a *commedia dell'arte* troupe, the "play" is about to begin. There is an air of mockery and satire in this scene so serious for Amón and so droll for Tamar. When the action oversteps the bounds of propriety, Tamar calls a halt to the "drama." As a result of the feigned love-making, Amón feels better probably because he participated seriously in the "play." And also because Tamar offered to pretend to be more in love with him than he was with his deceased princess. The difference is one of attitude toward the "play." Amón plays his role with all seriousness; Tamar considers the charade a "donosa aventura" (II, 754). Amón also feels better because he has now found an identity for himself, an identity which no other woman has been able to give him, "y, en fin, por ser con vos mucho / no vengo, Infanta, a ser nada" (I, 817-8). Amón needs not only the love of a woman but also the affection of his future subjects. He questions his servant Eliazer about their feelings, "¿Quiérenme mucho? (II, 31). Here is yet another sign of Amón's need for him.

After Tamar withdraws from the "play," Amón runs in desperation to his servant Jonadab for advice. It is in this scene that Tirso develops more fully the deterioration of love into pure sexual passion that points the way towards a violent and illicit sex act. Jonadab's scheme rests on the assumption that Amón's life is worth more than the loss of Tamar's honor. He knows that David dotes on Amón and will grant his every request. Tamar is to prepare food and feed Amón. Once Amón is alone with Tamar, the opportunity will dictate his actions. Before Jonadab leaves, Amón utters an important statement: love does not distinguish between people of color nor does it respect the relationship of brother and sister, probably because they are all man-made constraints.

Jonadab's remarks encourage Amón to justify rationally his irrational scheme to rape Tamar. Since like attracts like and brother and sister are alike in blood relationship, appearance and merit and equally worthy of each other's love, what law can prohibit what love ordains? Amón follows the law of nature and finds support in the examples of Adam's children who intermarried. Has Amón forgotten that Tamar loves Joab and will marry him for love? Amón's passion for Tamar undermines the love that he professes. Love is no longer a feeling of tenderness, caring and sharing, with mutual respect for one another but rather it will become cruel, brutal and a violent act that dehumanizes because it deprives one person of free choice. In Amón's thinking love is blind and gropes its way in the darkness of ignorance and irrationality just as it did in the garden when he was attracted by Tamar's singing. The climax of Act Two occurs when Amón forces Tamar to do his will. He compares love with appetite, a concept that rejects love as a feeling of tenderness and defames it, but degrading it to the level of beastiality, cruelty and violence.

After the defloration Amón's "love" turns to hate, a hatred now more intense than his former "love." He casts her aside like a disposable object, showing no remorse or self-reproach. In fact he blames her for the predicament metaphorically describing her as "veneno," "sepulcro," "arpía," "fiera," "basilisco" and "monstruo" (III, 2-9).

David turns down Tamar's plea for justice (=revenge) and pardons Amón out of love when the latter addresses his father in terms of endearment, "amoroso padre" and "piadoso padre" (III, 362; 364). Moved more by compassion than justice, David pardons Amón because he remembers how God pardoned his youthful misdeeds (III, 370-8).

At Balhasor Amón falls in love with a shepherdess, intrigued by the beauty of her eyes and hands.[4] When he discovers it is Tamar in disguise, he reviles her, calling her a monster and "afrenta de las mujeres" (III, 901). His uncontrollable passion leads to tragedy. In the closing moments of the play, Absalón kills Amón to avenge Tamar's dishonor as Amón subverts love by his cruelty, his lack of tenderness, his irrationality and his obsession with sex.

III

Tamar is engaged to marry Joab, a general in King David's army. Her lover being absent, Tamar creates an imagined reality expressed in the song "Ligero pensamiento" (I, 353 ff) and "Ay pensamiento" (I, 441 ff). In the song she wishes the bird drinking at the fountain in the garden would convey her pain to her lover over his absence. She gently reproves the bird for its celerity in leaving and its tardiness in returning. She experiences vicariously what she imagines the bird will encounter—the sight and sounds of her beloved. The key word in the song is "pensamiento," a word that depicts the reality of a rendezvous spawned and enacted in her thoughts. She plots the scenario in her mind including the situations and events the bird will encounter. Tirso describes her mind metaphorically as an oven in which she will bake the bread of tender thoughts about Joab, thus sustaining him against violent suspicion (I, 300 ff).

Her sisterly love that impels her to care for Amón in his illness could lead her to great lengths to restore him to health, "sabe Dios, gallardo hermano, / con cuanta solicitud / hierbas y piedra buscara, / experiencias aprendiera / montes ásperos subiera, / filósofos consultara / para volver a Israel / un príncipe que la muerte / quitalle pretende" (II, 495-503). Because he is her brother, she allows him to kiss her hands, a ritual he will pursue several times throughout the play, "por ser tu hermana consiento / los favores que me haces" (II, 521-2). After hearing his story about his love for an Ammonite princess now deceased, the compassionate Tamar is all the more affected by his plight, "me aflige más tu querella" (II, 664). She enthusiastically assents to play the role of a lover ardently and perhaps somewhat imprudently, "que en mí tu dama hallarás, / quizá más correspondiente / que la que ansí te abrasó" (II, 720-2). Perceiving her not as his sister but rather his inamorata, she plays her role with unbounded zest, "preténdeme diligente, / que con industrioso engaño / mientras tu hermana no soy, / para que sanes te doy" (II, 724-7).

On overhearing the rehearsal, Joab rebukes her for "amores abominables." Tamar explains that her 'love' for Amón was only an apparent "love" (II, 876). She contends that when a madman pretends to be king, one who is discreet humors him to extract oneself from an intolerable situation. Since Tamar knows the power of passion, she decided to indulge him so that little by little he might overcome his irrationality. She is quick to deny any intentional wrongdoing and agrees not only to stop the charade but also to seek Amón's death. Having been disillusioned by her love Joab for her "amores abominables," Tamar withdraws from Amón's charade. She is no longer his pretended "dama," only his sister; she is finished with deception and dissembling language (II, 963).

After the rape, Tamar is overcome by despair. Having lost her most prized possession, her virginity, she wonders what will become of her, for she knows that "mujer gozada es basura" (III, 29). In biblical times men only married women who were virgin. An unchaste woman was thrown into the streets to fend for herself (III, 30; 232). Seeking redress for grievances, Tamar appeals to David, hoping to move him to compassion just as she was compassionate with Amón's affliction. She complains of Amón's "amor desatinado" (III, 193-4). Asking for justice, and calling upon David to control his emotions and act as King rather than as father, Tamar would rather live among wild beasts by whom her honor would never be violated (III, 314 ff). Tamar's use of "mancha," "agua," "espejo," "agua/sangre" calls attention to her concern for her stained honor which now blocks the way to a marriage with Joab and becomes a virtual obsession, obliterating any trace of her once sisterly love.

Sadly, Tamar goes disguised as a shepherdess to Balhasor where the shepherds attempt to mitigate her melancholy with songs. Tirso, one of the shepherds, speaking for the dramatist of the same name, states what looms as a dominant theme, "Para agravios de honra, / perdón o venganza" (III, 678-9). If she is sad, time, the great physician, will heal all wounds. Unaware of her identity and moved by love and by the power of beauty, Amón tries to force his attentions on her. Tamar repulses him and repeats the verse that is to serve as an *estribillo*, "¡Qué amigo sois de forzar!" (III, 889 et passim). After Absalón kills Amón, Tamar feels exhilarated by revenge which has defeated love, albeit self-love, "ya podré mirar la gente, / resucitando mi honra, / que la sangre del traidor / es blasón del inocente" (III, 969-72). Whether she ever marries Joab is left to the reader's imagination. Tamar subverts love by her concern only for herself and her honor.

IV

Absalón's vaulting ambition to be ruler of Israel blots out any feeling of love he has either for his father or his brother Amón. He is vain, arrogant but shrewd, a brilliant conversationalist and a paragon of physical beauty that evokes feminine admiration. Although he is a philanderer, he disdains any one who is not in love. He compares courtship to war, "luego Amor a Morte iguala." Absalón uses the metaphor of love/war to justify his scaling the walls of a woman's abode. He creates another reality with his imagination, debasing love to the status of a military operation (I, 69-76). Absalón lives in a fantasy world fully aware of his physical attractiveness which he shares with all women (I, 90). He believes that beauty is the heart of the kingdom, "señal que es noble el alma que está en ella, / que el huésped bello habita en casa bella" (III, 142-3). His conclusion, of course, is a non-sequitur.

To accomplish his goal to rule Israel, Absalón must eliminate both his father and his brother. He argues that whoever cannot control his sexual appetite is not fit to govern. He sides with Tamar who seeks redress for her defilement. He is an opportunist who will take advantage of Tamar's plight to further his own ends and at the same time to avenge her dishonor.

Absalón's dream to rule is reflected in his insatiable desire to wear the crown which he sees lying on a platter one day. He crowns himself and finds it a tasty morsel not to be despised. For a brief moment he enjoys an imagined reality that has eluded him up to now. Talking to himself, he vows to kill all who would stand in his way: his brother and his father. When David, who has overheard the monologue, confronts Absalón with his own words, the latter invents a lie, twisting his words to mean that he would slay whoever would be a traitor to the King. When David asks who that might be, Absalón responds, slyly, "quien a su hermana forzó / también matará a su padre" (III, 468-9). Absalón swears he loves Amón more than anybody else in Israel. He invites David to Balhasor where he will be regaled, "conocerá que intereso / granjear sólo su amor" (III, 494-5). There a banquet, which could turn into a love-feast of family harmony and love, results in a bitter tragedy.

David urges Absalón to forget hate and pardon Amón; then he would be Abel instead of Cain (III, 496-9). Absalón hopes to hang by the hair of his head if he harms Amón. With this assurance David pardons his son's youthful follies. The astute Absalón challenges David to prove his love by allowing Amón to go to Balhasor. David follows his experience; he knows that rancor is no more dangerous than when it comes disguised as peace. Finally David grants his son's request but not without doubts and apprehension. Love, enmity and pardon again intrude on the ending when Absalón breaks his promise and slays Amón just as the latter broke his promise never to offend his father again when he tried to seduce Tamar a second time.

Absalón is depicted as a cold-blooded liar who would kill his father and brother to satisfy his ambition to rule. He swears falsely to his father that his love for Amón would not allow him to harm his eldest brother. Tirso paints the conflict between father and son with such bold contrasts and poignancy, the son being a manipulator and the father gullible and good-natured, that these scenes stand out as some of the highlights of the dramatic action and of the subversion of love by self-interest.

V

David is perhaps the most pathetic figure in the tragedy. Upon his return from battle, he manifests his love for his family and his concern for the well-being of all, especially his eldest son, Amón. David is deeply disturbed by Amón's spell of melancholy, his failure to comunicate and his inability to curb his imagination. The King is distressed by Amón's illness and longs for even a look or word of love: "¿aunque fingiéndolo fuera, / una palabra siquiera / de amor?" (II, 478-80). In his great love for his son, David has won many kingdoms which he would give Amón "por ser tú el hijo primero" (II 424).

After learning of Tamar's rape, David's love for his children begins to turn to disillusion, "¿Esto es, cielos, tener hijos?" (III, 284). In his judgment of Amón, the King is torn between justice and love, "Piedad sus ojos me piden, / la Infanta satisfacción" (III, 350-1). When Amón appears contrite and addresses him as "amoroso padre" and "piadoso padre," David is overcome with compassion (III, 362; 367). He remembers that God pardoned him for his adulterous behavior with Bathsheba and reasons that, "El castigo es mano izquierda, / mano es derecha el perdón" (III, 376-7). As a loving father, David utters no words of condemnation, only of advice (III, 379-80). Nor does he speak one word of sympathy for the wronged Tamar.

David is loathe to allow Amón to go to Balhasor with his brother for relaxation, fearful of an untoward incident. Absalón decides to test the father's love. Accepting Absalón's promise not to harm Amón, and full of misgivings, David challenges him, "lo mucho que te amo pruebas" (III, 555). In the closing moments of the play, David appears alone on stage awaiting the return of his sons. He longs to embrace Amón but his arms clasp only the air. He becomes more and more disillusioned as he addresses the " . . . engaños lisonjeros, / ¿Por qué con burlas pesadas / me hacéis abrazar los vientos?" (III, 996-8). In a series of analogues he mockingly derides love which has deluded him and brought him grief. David is uncertain about Amón's fate and wonders if he has been offered as a sacrificial lamb.[5]

VI

The imagination, a function of the mind, plays a major role in Amón's life on stage in subverting love. When he hears the sweet voice of a woman whose identity he does not yet know, his imagination concludes that the possessor of such a sweet voice must be beautiful, a *fallacia consequentis*. His imagination drafts a mental scenario in which he and Tamar are to play the role of lovers. Tamar agrees, convinced by his argument that love can be deceived and that human beings likewise can be deluded by the reality of the seemingly unreal. Amón's memory (another facet of the mind) stores the image of the deceased Ammonite princess; she was beautiful and he now transfers her likeness to Tamar, a second impossible love affair.

Amón does not have an identity. He loves many women but they all have physical flaws. He will not fall in love until he finds perfect beauty. He falls in love with Tamar's sweet voice and finally with her because she is the image of his deceased princess. Amón's mental health improves and he finds a new identity through an unreal love, "y en fin, por ser con vos mucho, / no vengo, Infanta, a ser nada" (I, 517-8).

The drama within a drama interlaces the serious and the comic: Amón plays his part with complete seriousness while Tamar considers the play a "donosa burla" but facetiously agrees to play her role to the hilt. There is no true love in the charade; it grants Amón only temporary relief. Since it is a feigned love, it holds no promise for continuity nor happiness in the future. It finally culminates in disaster.

The subversion of love is highlighted when the irrational controls the rational. The dramatist unobtrusively and skillfully interweaves the rational with the irrational. Amón refuses to go on a whoring expedition with his brothers but goes out on his own after they have left. He conceives the plan to rape Tamar and then blames her. Absalón wants to punish Amón for raping Tamar; his concealed motive is to eliminate a rival for the throne. Absalón advises Tamar to choose reason over emotion and avoid vengeance (III, 295-7). Amón's attempt to justify his intended rape of Tamar leads him to rationalize that like attracts like and that if brother and sister find affection for each other this love should not be subject to man-made restrictions; in this he chooses to follow "natural law."

Amón's concept of love turns to outright lust, thus causing an imbalance which subverts love. He kisses Tamar's hand several times throughout the play and her mouth and lips. When he cannot fulfill his desire, he resorts to violence, deceit and cruelty and forces his will on Tamar. After the seduction he abuses her with vile names and repulsive metaphors that reflect his intense hatred. Amón insists he follows "Natural Law" rather than man-made law which deprives him of love (II, 1017-19). But in Amon's concept of love there is no place for compassion, understanding, tenderness of feeling, trust, fidelity and caring and sharing. These ideas stand in the shadows of pleasure and honor, the twin springs of subversion in the tragedy.

All four main characters suffer the pain of a counterfeit love. Absalón loves to rule. He falsely swears he loves his father and brother; he kills Amón and would kill his father. Tamar loves her honor to the point where it becomes an obsession for which she would be an accomplice to murder. David's love for Amón is so great that the youth knows how to manipulate the father and get away with rape. Amón subverts love by translating it in terms of lust.

Chapter 6

Tirso's Perception and Portrayal of a Rapist

The Spanish *comedia*'s insight into the working of the human mind and its effects on feelings, emotions and behavior is one of the hallmarks of its greatness. I have already investigated a segment of this area in an earlier study (see my essay, "The Comedia as a Theater of the Mind"). The present chapter will examine Tirso's perception of a sexual obsession that portrays the protagonist Amón as a rapist in *La venganza de Tamar*. It will attempt to answer such questions as: what are the circumstances that aid and abet Amón's obsession? What stimuli influence his compulsion? How does Tirso depict them? The essay will trace Tirso's perception of Amón's sexual fixation as a product of the mind in its several functions: memory, imagination, reason and feelings.

Amón, eldest son of King David and heir to the throne, turns out to be a complex character as A. K. G. Paterson has already noticed (15). As the play opens his servant Eliazer can understand why Amón would hate war but is puzzled by the prince's aversion to love. Amón responds, "Cosa es nueva" (I, 40), explaining that only the one who invents something new is worthy of esteem. He characterizes himself as "singular." This striving for recognition indicates that he has not yet established a stable identity. His younger brother Absalón uses the traditional metaphor of love and war. In both activities men scale the walls, patrol them day and night and plan strategies.

Perceiving Amón's envy of his beauty, Absalón plants into his brother's pliable mind an idea that will obsess him to the ultimate tragedy, "la hermosura es perfección, / y lo perfecto es amable" (I, 87-8). Amón cannot compete with Absalón's natural beauty nor with his conversational ability. His envy displays itself even more forcefully when he ridicules his brother's long golden hair, which functions as a sex symbol since it attracts women to him. Amón has not loved any one woman among the many he has been courting; he has found physical defects in all.

Eliazer suggests tauntingly that he make a perfect woman of clay and be another Pygmalion. This he will do in his mind, creating the image of a beautiful woman and associating it with physical beauty. Amón will never love, "tengo mala condición" (I, 144). His brother asks if he will attend the wedding festivities for Josefo and Elisa. Amón will go but rather unwillingly, and masked to observe the bride's beauty. Absalón wonders how Amón could consider the bride beautiful if he has never been in love. The conversation about love and beauty affects Amón's thinking; he perceives himself to be neither handsome nor a good speaker. This creates a feeling of inferiority. Moreover, he has not found a beautiful woman who meets his expectations.

Amón is seemingly shocked by Absalón's brazen invitation to join him in courting David's concubines (I, 184-6). He cannot be considered mindless when he offers the discerning observation that, "la belleza y la locura / son hermanas; eres bello, / y estás loco . . . " (I, 193-5). He is reluctant to speak of his love and believes that it should be kept secret. Therefore, he refuses to join his brother in a whoring expedition.

After his brothers have left, Amón decides to scale the walls of his father's harem in search of an erotic encounter. He speaks disparagingly of women as a "frágil sujeto," and "un animal imperfecto" (I, 226-7) before his servants Jonadab and Eliazer. They encourage him with philosophical vagaries to satisfy his sexual dreams. One cautions him about invading his father's domain. But Amón is adamant; once his mind is made up fourteen preachers will be unable to persuade him to the contrary (I, 286-90).

As he approaches the harem wall, he hears the beautiful voice of Tamar, whose identity he will not learn until Act Two. He falls in love with the voice and its owner, reasoning that whoever possesses such a beguiling voice must be beautiful. In his imagination he has begun to form a vague concept of his amorous quest, "¿Quién duda que es hermosa? / ¿quién duda que conviene / su cara con su canto?" (I, 411-13). The imagination creates a mental image, a picture of what he hopes to find on the other side of the wall; it also arouses in him a feeling of exhilaration. Mary Warnock maintains that the imagination also controls the feelings.

Fascinated by the singing of a mythical siren and applying the message of the song to himself, Amón loses his balance on the wall and falls. Tamar helps him to his feet, and in gratitude he kisses her hand ardently. From Tamar's conversation with her servant Dina, Amón knows that she will be wearing a red dress to the wedding tomorrow.

The idea of love is further imprinted on his mind when the wedding party approaches; Tamar is attired in a red dress, the sight of which fans the flames of Amón's passion. After recognizing her as his half-sister, he becomes frustrated and angry. But only momentarily, for his passion has been revived and he cannot escape its inexorable tyranny. Like so many other protagonists in Golden Age drama, he recognizes his weakness but can do little about it, since we now know that the passions spring from the unconscious, as Jung pointed out.

Screening his identity behind a mask and a cloak, Amón brazenly displays his arrogance by admitting to Tamar that he was the one who had kissed her hand. He feels that he is being persecuted and in fact he is, but by a power he is unable to control and does not understand. He is besieged by contrary desires and emotions that make up his nature (I, 810). Jung explains this division in the personality as the result of the conscious mind's desire to cling to its moral ideals while the unconscious mind struggles after its unmoral ideal which the conscious mind tries to deny (Jung, *Two essays*, 20).

Amón, cognizant of his " . . . imposibles desvelos," curses the garden where he first met Tamar, and the madness that forced him to scale the walls at the behest of a domineering Cupid (I, 685). His superego tells him to forget, to remain silent and die, but his ego, which he describes as "mi locura vana," "el tormento . . . más atroz" and " . . . la pasión más tirana," impels him to continue with his scheme (I, 715-16). His conscience teeters on the brink of despair as it tells him he is a monster of impossibilities.

As Act Two opens it is obvious that Amón needs the love of many people, to judge by the poignancy of his question, "¿Quiérenme mucho?" (II, 31). Another servant, Jonadab, assures him that all Jerusalem is concerned about his melancholy. Eliazer's long account of some physicians' sexual promiscuity keeps the idea of illicit sex fresh in Amón's mind. Since his sexual problems have not been solved, Amón feels out of sorts. He has failed to come to terms with his emotional problems which he attributes to "enemigos invisibles" (II, 223). These invisible enemies are the antagonistic forces (love/lust) which are struggling for control of the mind. The memory of a beautiful princess haunts him and constantly rekindles his passion.

David's triumphant return has little impact on Amón who is now so overcome by melancholy that he only wants to be alone with his thoughts. Robert Burton theorized that "the passions are linked to the imagination and men carried away with passion are not only melancholic but quite mad, and devoid of reason" (40). It is tempting indeed to diagnose Amón's ailment in modern terms as "manic-depressive psychosis" (S. Jackson), but it should also be kept in mind that melancholia was a fashionable malady in seventeenth century Europe.

The sight of Tamar again arouses his languishing spirit and inflames his passion. He detects in Tamar's naïveté and compassion a way to satisfy his sexual craving. It is at this juncture that we reach a "branching point," as David Gitlitz calls it, where we can decide whether Amón is preparing furtively for the rape he intends, or is just "playing" at love much the way children play games. I select the first of the two alternatives because in my opinion Amón is a schemer who plots the scenario of his intended "drama" in his head and then slowly but cunningly persuades the unwary Tamar to engage in sexual promiscuity at a time when she is already engaged to Joab. What Amón wants is not illusion but reality and he thinks he can find reality through illusion.

Amón in desperation takes Tamar into his confidence, revealing how he fell in love with a beautiful Ammonite princess who perished in the siege of the city. He is desperate because he still loves her, carrying her image in his memory. He realizes now that it is an impossible love; the only way to assuage his feelings is to pretend that she is still here, and this he does by transferring her image on to Tamar. He proposes an improvised play: Tamar will enact the role of his "dama," and he will be her "galán." This will all be done on the pretext of restoring Amón to health. He argues that Love (Cupid) is a child; a child can easily be deceived by anything feigned. This is the way he intends to deceive the naïve but charitable Tamar. How does Tirso accomplish this?

Tirso has Amón marshal four analogues to buttress his thesis and convince Tamar that his love problem can be appeased by an artful deception. The play within a play was a favorite device of the seventeenth century Spanish dramatists and, according to Lionel Abel, it presents a new view of dramatic form. But in Amón's hands it reaches another dimension of diabolical trickery: it becomes a means to destroy an unsuspecting victim. Amón deceives her with the notion "que sin que llegue al manjar, / le satisfaga la mesa" (II, 699-700). He reassures her that, because of their blood relationship, no untoward incident can occur. Convinced now that feigned love is the medicine Amón needs, Tamar guilelessly encourages him to express his sexual desires. Tamar is carried away by the novelty and excitement of the 'play.' In her unsophistication she offers to play the role to the hilt, "que en mí tu dama hallarás, / quizá más correspondiente / que la que te abrasó" (II, 720-22).

The 'play' that Amón has conceived in his imagination takes place on two levels, the serious and the comic placed in juxtaposition for greater ironic effect. Amón is deadly serious; Tamar takes the "play" as a joke, " . . . donosa aventura, / comienzo a hacer mi figura; / no haré poco en no reírme" (II, 754-56), and "donosas burlas . . . " (II, 803). The "play" must observe certain parameters beyond which it cannot go. When the action becomes too realistic, Tamar, despite her naïveté, cautions him, "las leyes de hermano pasas" (II, 795). The prince is momentarily thwarted and summons her to a rendezvous that evening. Joab, Tamar's lover, who has overheard the "play," warns Tamar that she is jeopardizing their forthcoming marriage and their honor. Tamar is convinced and agrees to desist.

Later, Tamar informs Amón that she no longer wants "palabras disfrazadas" and "engaño" but an honorable marriage to Joab. The "play" is over and Amón must now seek other means to attain his ends. He is not long in finding them. His friend Jonadab proposes a scheme whereby Amón is to go to bed pretending illness. Amón believes the solution is in the proposal, arguing falsely in a sonnet the thesis, "¿qué ley impide lo que amor alcanza?" (II, 1013). The arguments in the sonnet are ingeniously arranged starting with the notion that "amor consiste en semejanza," followed by an appeal to "natural law." Here Tirso cleverly demonstrates how the power to reason can be used to justify an impending immoral act.

The unsuspecting David grants Amón's seemingly modest request. After David leaves, Eliazer sings a short, lyrical song on the theme of love as a kind of prelude to what will follow. Again this keeps the topic of love in the foreground of Amón's consciousness. Obediently, Tamar comes to warn Amón about the scheme he has in mind, for that kind of love " . . . no estará sazonado" (II, 1078). As the act draws to a close, Amón argues, speciously again, "No hay amor injusto," and "para amor no hay ley" (II, 1105-6). What Amón does not realize is that he is unable to distinguish love from lust as Pallarés Navarro has observed in this and other Tirsian plays.

As Act Three opens, Amón has raped Tamar and has discarded her like a disposable object. What was once "love" has now turned to hate, probably because what he perceived to be "love" was only carnal desire. Dressed in mourning, Tamar pleads for justice before David, but in vain. After she withdraws, Amón appears and addresses his father in endearing terms, "amoroso padre," and "piadoso padre" (III, 362, 367). His words may be read either as filial affection or as an act of obsequiousness. Remembering how God pardoned his sins, David reasons, "el castigo es mano izquierda, / mano es derecha el perdón" (III, 376-7). Soon thereafter Amón vows never again to offend his father's love, a pledge he will in time violate.

Later when it is sheep-shearing time on the country estate in Balhasor, Amón catches sight of a beautiful shepherdess with alluring eyes and hands. Forgetting the promise he made, he forcibly grabs her hands. Unwilling to have the wool pulled over her eyes, Tamar remarks, "¡Qué amigo sois de forzar!" (III, 873; 889; 897). When he discovers Tamar's identity, Amón reviles her as a monster. Later at dinner Absalón kills Amón to avenge Tamar's dishonor.

In conclusion, Tirso's insight into the workings of the human mind and his knowledge of Faculty Psychology enabled him to portray graphically the rapist Amón as he perceived him in *La venganza de Tamar*. He argues that Amón's pliant and receptive mind is influenced by external stimuli that assault him: a woman's voice, the darkness of the night, Tamar's love-song addressed to a bird, and the sultry weather. He adds other references that constantly keep the question of sex in the center of Amón's attention.

Tirso introduces songs of a highly lyrical nature to prefigure an upcoming climactic scene. He intersperses sonnets at points of crisis and his use of different verse forms creates a pervasive atmosphere of sexuality. References to various parts of the human anatomy: hair, hands and eyes suggest the physical aspect of love and lust and keep the theme of sex ever before Amón. Besides these external influences, there are also internal ones. These exist mainly in Amón's mind and relate to memory, imagination, emotion and reason. Amón is driven by an impossible dream: perfection in an imperfect world. His imagination enables him to fashion a perfect speciman of feminine beauty, an illusion that compensates for his inability to confront reality.

Tirso shows that Amón suffers persecution by invisible enemies. These exist only in his mind and result from his failure to reconcile the conflicting forces of emotion and reason in his psyche. To satisfy an emotional need, he exploits Tamar's goodness of heart, relying on her naïveté and compassion and inveigling her to yield by a sly trick conceived in his imagination. Tirso depicts how an obsession expressed by metaphors, lies and objects constantly dangled before Amón remains in his consciousness, and directs his thinking toward sex.

The dramatist skillfully depicts a mind divided between love and lust struggling with the concept until one overcomes the other. He employs the popular device of a play within a play which, in Amón's hands, becomes a lethal weapon to destroy the life of a charitable and good-natured half-sister by luring her unsuspectingly toward an act of depravity. Tirso perceives Amón as a scoundrel driven by an uncontrollable erotic passion and portrays him as a manipulator of people for his own ends.

Tirso demonstrates that the excessive love of a doting father and his act of forgiveness toward his son are no guarantee that the later will not repeat his crime. Pardoned but never punished or reprimanded, Amón is beguiled by the hands and eyes of a shepherdess whom he attempts to rape. The intended victim turns out to be Tamar in disguise.

Amón employs the power to reason, contrive and justify an anti-social act rather than to discriminate between good and evil, love and lust. He denigrates women and reduces the rapist to the level of a beast, thus dehumanizing himself and the human race. Amón is a sly and crafty rascal who entices a naïve, well-meaning victim to dishonor built on the reality of illusion and the illusion of reality.

The playwright dramatically and poetically reveals the working of a mind obsessed by an erotic passion under the control of the irrational which passes for the rational. Tirso brilliantly displays his ability to dramatize the clash and interaction of opposites in a play long neglected, probably because of the repugnance of the themes of rape and incest.

Chapter 7

Deconstructing *La venganza de Tamar*

A. K. G. Paterson in his edition of Tirso's *La venganza de Tamar*, states that it is a "drama about justice" (14).[1] This chapter will scrutinize those aspects of Tirso's notions about justice not examined by Paterson; in doing so it will take up Tirso's dramatic techniques in deferring the main theme of justice until the third act where it moves to the foreground and replaces that of rape (and incest). It will also investigate the struggle for supremacy between pardon and punishment by considering an intrusive element in the equation and exposing its different connotations arising from the dramatist's concept of justice.

Like other approaches to literary criticism, the New Criticism, semiotics, reader response and sociological, deconstruction requires a close reading of the text. It deals with the science of signs and their multiple meanings as has been demonstrated by Saussure, Derrida, Culler, Miller, Norris and others. Unlike the New Criticism, deconstruction does not seek to find the only, correct meaning of a text. The polysemic nature of a sign not only shifts the focus to multiplicity of meanings but also transfers the burden from the author to the reader who becomes a partner in creativity. Catherine Belsey declares that the text does not provide the meaning as something already made by the author, but it is the reader who determines the meaning of the text (134-5). The deconstructionist critic abandons the idea of finding one truth or one meaning, and by studying a recurring image, a central theme, an unusual characterization, or some verbal aspect lays the foundation for an analysis.

The plot of *Venganza* is deceptively simple and drives from the story of Amón's rape of Tamar as found in 2 Sam (2 Kings) 13. But in the play there is more than meets the eye. For two acts it treats of Amón's lust for a beautiful woman, even if it leads to rape. Amón, who has fallen in love with a beautiful Ammonite princess who perished in the war, now sees her image reflected in his half-sister Tamar whom he begins to court. Realizing it is an impossible love, Amón falls into a spell of dejection. To alleviate his melancholy, Amón proposes that they enact a "play" about his love for the dead beauty. After some discussion the charitable Tamar agrees to participate. By this substitution for reality, Amón hopes to achieve his goal of copulating with her. She, however, stops the charade when it comes too close to reality. At first Amón wins the sympathy of the reader who views him as a victim of an uncontrollable passion until he resorts to trickery to seduce Tamar; at that point he loses reader rapport. What seemed to be erotic love in the beginning now turns to lust which must be satisfied at any cost. At first Tamar's love for her brother is based on family ties, but after the seduction her love turns to hate as does Amón's but for different reasons: one for satiety, the other for dishonor. This reversal typifies another characteristic of deconstruction: the binary opposition here reflected by *amor/desamor*.

After the defilement the drama enters into its most important phase in which the reader is challenged to provide the meaning. It is not just a question of rape and incest and how Amón (with Jonadab's help) will consummate the crime, but what action the powers that be will take in this situation, why and under the guidance of what philosophy? Tamar has to plead her case before King David. The monarch has to bear in mind that in those days incest and rape were prohibited by law and any violation was subject to prosecution (Leviticus 18-19). The noted biblical scholar Gerald Larue recalls that Ezekiel, who was writing during the sixth century B. C., condemned sexual relations between brother and sister (Ezek 22:11) (94-5). He also refers to Deuteronomy 27:22 which records a cursing ritual for incest.[2] The prohibition against rape and incest continued in Christian Spain during the Middle Ages according to the several *Fueros* that Marjorie Ratcliffe has examined (94).

Tamar is well aware of the social consequences of her plight, "Mujer gozada es basura" (III, 29). Ostracized by society, she will be cast into the street to fend for herself (III, 42-5). Pleading her case, she hopes to move the King to compassion (III, 180-183). She emphasizes how Amón has stained the royal honor which can only be cleansed by the shedding of blood (III, 242). She begs the King to be guided by justice (reason) rather than by passion (mercy), "véncete Rey a ti mismo, / la justicia a la pasión" (III, 260-1).

David is torn between justice and compassion as he listens to Tamar's arguments (III, 176-78). Absalón beseeches Tamar unsuccessfully to let reason overcome her desire for revenge, offering to care for her at his country estate in Balhasor. When Absalón comments, "Puertas adentro se quede / mi agravio y tu deshonor," is he thinking of the notion of "a secreto agravio, secreta venganza," (III, 300-1)? Does he mean to cover up the crime and remain silent? Further on Absalón tries to console Tamar with the idea that time heals everything and her sorrow will be alleviated by her capacity to forget (III, 310-13). The other brothers are appalled by the crime. Adonías cannot find consolation in words; Salomón regrets the incident.

Trembling on the threshhold of the judgment hall, Amón considers David's silvery hair as the vestige of a fire long extinguished, the cold ashes of a once burning love. As he kneels at a distance out of fear and respect, David ponders his decision. Will it be based on justice or affection? Should family ties interfere with the dispensing of justice? Moreover, what will Israel say if he is remiss in his obligation to the state? The reader is left to consider whether Amón speaks out of contrition or out of self-interest, hoping to take advantage of his father's loving and kind disposition when he addresses him as, "amoroso padre," and "piadoso padre" (III, 362, 367).

The loving words strike a responsive chord as David now remembers how God pardoned him for previous misconduct as when he sent Uriah to his death. Then he could marry Bathesheba, an affair that began as an act of adultery (2 Sam 11). Bringing the analogy to bear on the present situation, David reasons, "Venció en ál a la justicia / la piedad. Su imagen soy, / El castigo es mano izquierda, / mano es derecha el perdón" (III, 374-7). The key ideas in David's thinking are, 1) pardon, and 2) no punishment. The King's thought may dwell on the figurative meaning of "izquierdo" as "twisted." Is Amón impressed by David's warning, "que mirase por mí dijo / blandamente me avisó. / El castigo del prudente / es la tácita objeción" (III, 386-9)? Does the second verse imply that David's face expressed disappointment over his son's misbehavior and that he thought it best not to exacerbate Amón's feelings at this time? Or that the most prudent form of punishment was an unspoken rebuke? Amón is so overwhelmed by his father's love and magnanimity that he vows never to offend him again, a pledge he soon breaks (III, 858-905).

The question of intertextuality, a major concern of deconstruction, arises when we recall that Tirso reworked the biblical text by inserting the idea of justice tempered by love, which is lacking in the original. Tirso redefines justice which will occupy the rest of the drama and eclipse the themes of rape and incest. The dramatist is not expressing a new idea since many of the OT signs point to their reintroduction in the NT, especially regarding the concepts of justice and love. It is at this point that the text is no longer restricted to a single, harmonious and authoritative reading when David violates the Hebrew tradition of an "eye for an eye." It now becomes plural, open to other readings. It is no longer an object for passive comsumption but rather one from which the reader can produce meaning.

The themes of rape and incest now move to the background and the reader's attention is drawn more and more to a concept of justice that includes a feeling of compassion together with a sense of fairness, of adjusting conflicting claims and the assignment of merited rewards or punishments. This shift in thematic centrality sharpens the dramatic conflict and at the same time it fleshes out the chracterization of David, who now occupies center stage because of his new interpretation of justice as mercy and compassion, attributes of love.

Absalón is shocked by his father's decision to pardon Amón, "¿que una razón no le dijo / en señal de sus enojos? / Ni un severo mirar de ojos?" (III, 394-6), thus suggesting no physical punishment. Absalón reasons that the father is blinded by the "pasión de amor," and that he (Absalón) will have to take matters into his own hands to redress the injustice done Tamar.[3] He concludes that "no es bien que reine en el mundo / quien no reina en su apetito" (III, 404-5), forgetting for a moment his own intemperate ambition to rule. The immediate referent is David but could it not also apply to Amón, which would be a justification for his future demise? Absalón may be second in line for the throne but, "ya por sus culpas," he considers himself "primero" (III, 409). The *sus* is polysemic; it can refer to "his" (Amón) and "their" (Amón and David).

Is it fair that Tamar be dishonored by the criminal act of rape without being compensated for the loss of her honor? Being a woman, is she any less worthy of remuneration than a man for the damage to her reputation? Absalón expects at least an angry David casting glances of reproach or even verbally admonishing his wayward son.

Closely allied to justice is the theme of love and its opposite, hate (*amor/desamor*). Absalón claims to love his father (III, 532-3), yet he would kill him to usurp the throne. He begs his father to test his love by allowing Amón to accompany him to the country estate at Balhasor. Are Absalón and Tamar in league to entice Amón to Balhasor where they can find "debida satisfacción?" (III, 321).

At Balhasor the shepherds, on learning of Tamar's dishonor, sing to console her. The theme in one of the verses turns on a binary opposition, "Para agravios de honor / perdón o venganza" (III, 678-9). Amón attempts to rape Tamar again but is deterred when he discovers her identity. At dinner Absalón slays Amón "por dar venganza a Tamar" (III, 940).

Tirso thus concludes his drama with a conventional ending: the criminal pays with his life for the crime he has committed. Justice is served and Tamar is avenged through hate. But Tirso has deftly injected another element to be considered in the concept of justice: love in its various meanings. Not only does David pardon Amón through love but Amón himself attempts to justify his intended rape of Tamar through "love." He bases his argument on Jonadab's comment that love is blind and cannot tell the difference between brother and sister. If like attracts like and no distinction can be made between brother and sister, and since they are alike in blood and worthy of each other's devotion, "¿qué ley impide lo que amor alcanza?" (II, 1013). This idea may seem logical but it is subversive and a daring challenge to the Hebrew law against incest. Moreover, Amón argues that to prohibit love between brother and sister would be contrary to Nature (II, 1019).[4] Several implications of love now loom large and excite the reader to search for a deeper meaning of the play.

The ascendancy of the theme of justice is delayed until Act Three because structurally the more profound meaning cannot be revealed until after certain events have taken place: David's pardon of Amón and Amón's demise by Absalón's hand. Thus two antagonistic ways of dispensing justice and showing love are open to interpretation by the reader.

Tamar considers Amón's death a fair price to pay for the restoration of her honor, "ya podré mirar la gente, / resucitando mi honor, / que la sangre del traidor / es blasón del inocente" (III, 969-72). Gerald Larue would agree, stating that "the death of

Amón puts the scales of Israelite justice in balance, so to speak" (104).

Back in Jerusalem, David suffers hallucinations: he imagines seeing Amón return. He goes to embrace his favorite son but his arms feel only the air. He recalls Absalón's promise not to harm Amón. Beseiged by hope and fear, the old man invokes Heaven in legal terminology to disillusion him (III, 1035-38). On receiving word of Amón's death, David weeps and mourns, attributing the tragedy to a "fiera pésima" (III, 1066).

At the end of the drama the reader is faced with more questions than answers. Does the punishment fit the crime? Which is a more just solution: pardon without punishment or revenge? What is Tirso's purpose in writing this play? Is it to show the barbarity and cruelty of the honor code of biblical times and also of his day? Does he wish to condemn the violence of the Hebraic law which demanded an "eye for an eye"? Against this backdrop Tirso unobtrusively weaves into his dramatic fabric the suggestion that pardon based on love and compassion may be the only just solution. Paterson perceives this and embodies it in the symbolism of the Slain Lamb as a representation of Christ's atonement for the sins of the world (24).[5] In the play hate wins and the question is raised: is hate a more powerful emotion than love?

The play underlines the inferior position of women in a male dominated society. After Tamar withdraws from the "play," Amón, who did not expect such a rejection, is depressed and turns to his friend Jonadab for a solution. The latter demands the status of women by suggesting a plan whereby Amón can save his life, which is worth more than Tamar's honor (II, 901-2). After David pardons Amón, why does the King pay no heed to Tamar's plea for justice, nor even offer her one word of sympathy? Did Tamar inform David of her fears concerning her preparation of food for Amón? Did David brush aside her concerns, thinking that her fears were unfounded and that she should now obey her father's order?

Why does David allow Amón to go to Balhasor, knowing of Absalón's passion to govern? Has David forgotten overhearing Absalón's scheme to kill him in order to ascend the throne? Does David choose to believe Absalón's love because it is in the nature of his character to be loving and kind? John Lyon contends that this points up David's weakness and gullibility (31). Does David find it necessary to show his confidence in Absalón's love, " . . . en fe de que me fío / de ti, yo te lo concedo" (III, 548-

9)? Absalón is now sure of his father's love, which he had doubted before, "de la poca fe me espanto / que tiene mi amor contigo" (III, 532-3). Is Absalón, like Amón, counting on David's great love for his children to accede to every request and then take full advantage of it for his own purposes?

Tirso presents the reader with several possible interpretations of the concept of justice. It is an issue that confronts people everywhere to this day. The problem of rape and incest and how they are chartered occupy the first two acts. The third broaches the problem of justice and produces a climax so intense and so pregnant with meaning that it becomes the overriding issue of the drama. The unusual characterization of David is depicted in such a way as to make it open to several interpretations. Both the central themes of justice and love and the unusual characterization of David contain an inherent ambiguity which defies a definitive interpretation and opens the way for other readings.

Notes

Chapter One

¹ Paterson's observations are found scattered in the "Introduction" and in the notes to his edition of the play.

² See my study on the "Imaginación."

³ Tirso impregnates the text with sensuality even in anecdotes that seemingly have nothing to do with the action. Eliazer repeats a story he heard a servant girl relate from a conversation she overheard. Six doctors had been summoned to care for a sick member of the family. Because of their profession, they enjoyed the freedom to practice illicit sexual acts with the women of the household, single and married. The interpolated anecdote reinforces the theme of illicit sexual relations of the main action.

⁴ The wall supposedly protects David's concubines against romantic assaults. Amón has accepted the concept of equality between love and war and points out his warlike attitude vis-à-vis love, especially in its destructive aspect.

⁵ On nudity, Cirlot opines that a nude (man or woman) always has ambivalent meanings. On the one hand it raises thought to the height of physical beauty and to the understanding of spiritual beauty. On the other, it can never lose its irrational attraction rooted in the biologic impulse beyond the control of the conscious mind.

⁶ S. G. Morley has found "encarnado" in *La república al revés* in the sense of "cruel."

⁷ The sphinx is a fabled animal composed of various parts of the human and animal body. According to Cirlot, it is the expression of an enigma whose ultimate meaning remains beyond human understanding.

⁸ Tirso employs the same concept of "fuego/agua" in *El burlador de Sevilla*. At first, Tisbea takes D. Juan for one who will bring the fire of love, "mucho fuego prometéis" (619). But now that he has disappeared, she describes him and herself with marine imagery, "nube que del mar salió / para anegar mis entrañas" (1010-1). Thus water like fire has both positive and negative aspects: it can give and destroy life and love. See my essay "Símbolos sexuales."

⁹ The zone is the term assigned to each one of the circles that encompass the sphere of heaven. The sign indicates one of the twelve sections in which a zone is divided and over which the Zodiac presides (Cirlot).

Chapter Two

1 Ovid in Book I of the *Metamorphoses*, "The Creation" described the strife between the four elements air, water, fire and earth. When completed, there was peace and harmony. His long poem is a poetic history from the creation to his day.

2 Tirso inverts the idea in *El burlador de Sevilla* where he has D. Juan emerge from the sea, having been shipwrecked and rescued by Catalinón. He brings love and new life to Tisbea who has heretofore disdained all her suitors. See Capítulo Segundo, "Simbolismo sexual en *El burlador*" in my book, *La mujer como víctima en la comedia y otros ensayos*, no. 11, p. 53.

3 Tirso uses the element water as a mirror elsewhere: III, 607-9; 630-41.

4 Amón describes his condition: "Sangre encierran otras venas; / en las mías todo es fuego" (II, 515-16). And again, "que si la sangre, en fin, sin fuego hierve, / ¿qué hará sangre que tiene tanto fuego?" (II, 1021-2).

5 According to Cirlot, the wall symbolizes an enclosure against danger from the outside. It is therefore a feminine symbol that signifies protection and security like a mother protecting her children.

6 The Sirens was Homer's term for the magic women of Cyrene whose "sweet song" lured Odysseus's sailors into shallow waters where their ships were wrecked on the rocky coast. Cirlot defines the siren as a symbolic figure that usually takes one of two main forms: "as a bird-woman or as a fish-woman" (297).

Tradition has it that woman represents the spirit of the earth as a temptress, and is constantly enticing man (who is the son of heaven) and dragging him to earth and destruction.

7 The earth is the agent that awakens everything to life. Everything springs from the earth and ends in the earth. "Earth derives from the Sanskrit *Artha*, "mater-ial wealth," the Latin *mater* means "mother" which becomes English "matter." (Walker).

8 According to Cirlot, a garden is a "place where Nature is subdued, ordered, selected and enclosed."

9 David's conquest of the lion and the bear is found in 1 Sam xvii (Lyon, 34-7).

Chapter Three

1 Some years ago Arnold G. Reichenberger pointed out that the two most important themes in the *comedia* were "la honra" and "la fe." He considered these as obstacles to the universal acceptance of the *comedia*. Some years later Eric Bentley, one of the best-known drama critics, indicated that Reichenberger had forgotten the importance of love as another principal theme of the *comedia*. I would add a fourth: deception, which appears in the vast majority of *comedias* as a theme and also as a dramatic device to advance the action.

Chapter Four

[1] In a section on Tirso, A. A. Parker discusses the philosophy of love in several plays. *La venganza de Tamar* is not included. His conclusion is that beauty sparks love. In *La venganza* it is beauty that forces Amón to love "pues su hermosura me esfuerza" (III, 871).

[2] These are the analogues: "Llora un niño, y a su ama / pide leche, y dale el pecho / tal vez otra sin provecho, / donde creyendo que mama / solamente se entretiene / ¿No has visto fingidas flores / que en apariencia y colores / la vista a engañarse viene? / Juega con la espada negra / en paz quien la guerra estima, / engañando con la esgrima / las armas con que se alegra. / Hambriento he yo conocido / que de partir y trinchar / suele más harto quedar / que los otros que han comido" (II, 673-88).

[3] As Paterson has observed, David suffered much under the Law and in his psalms he longs for the day when he will be redeemed from the Law.

Paterson maintains that he is not identifying Amón with Christ. David's idea of pardon points the direction that his notion will take in the hands of Christian theologians. Tirso inserted the idea into the tragedy because he knew that David spoke of pardon in the psalms. The idea of pardon was not very popular in that day because it denied a basic Hebrew notion—an eye for an eye—the *lex talionis*. Absalón clearly perceives that his father is blinded by paternal love and pardons Amón without punishing him and without a single word of reprimand. On the other hand, David does not sympathize with Tamar and her dishonor. Not a single word of compassion for her. Perhaps because she was a woman, she was worth nothing. This is also Amón's attitude after the seduction.

Chapter Five

[1] There is another edition of the play published recently by John Lyon which follows Paterson's text with a few minor alterations.

[2] There is more ridicule of women in II, 59: "(que bastaba ser mujer)."

[3] Another instance occurs in I, 651-3: "Vea vuestro sol un día, / y sepa yo si igualáis / la cara a la melodía."

[4] A. A. Parker has observed that it is the power of beauty that forces one to love. Amón tries to take the hand of the unidentified shepherdess, explaining, "llegaréosla yo a tomar, / pues su hermosura me esfuerzas" (III, 870-1).

[5] Did Tirso have in mind Abraham's willingness to sacrifice his son Isaac, where at the last moment God intervened and a lamb was offered in his place? Tamar makes a comparison between Isaac and Amón: the former was innocent, the latter was not (III, 252-7).

Chapter Seven

[1] Elsewhere Paterson expands his idea of *La venganza*, stating that it is a "drama about guilt, justice and mercy" (22).

[2] The penalties for violation of the incest law range from excommunication, a cursing ritual, to death (Larue, 94).

[3] Elsewhere David is so blinded by love for Amón that he would accept even a token sign of his "love" (II, 474-81).

[4] The idea of "natural love" is found in the following quotation,
> Perdone, pues la ley que mi amor priva,
> vedando que entre hermanos se conserva,
> que la ley natural en contra alego
> (II, 1017-10)

Paterson speaks of the "unnatural love" between brother and sister (13).

[5] Paterson acknowledges in a note that sheep-shearing does not imply slaughtering them, and denies identifying Amón with Christ, but apparently the thought had crossed his mind (24). In my view the sheep and the shepherds present a bucolic setting of peace and tranquility broken only by the festive songs to contrast with the disarray in David's family and the subsequent violent deaths of Amón and Absalón.

There are, of course, other possible interpretations of the sheep-shearing metaphor. After the shearing, the sheep will live. After David pardons Amón, the son will live, but only a short time, until he forgets his pedge never to offend his father's love again. Then he will become a victim to propitiate the Gods as "de sus esquilmos cordero" (III, 1022). David fears for his son's life, that his son will be the sacrificial lamb slain on the altar of revenge to appease those who would play God in administering justice.

Another possible reading revolves around the loss of virginity. Tamar is threatened by rape a second time, but this time the "shearing" does not take place as Amón desists on learning her identity. Tirso continues the metaphor by applying it to love and expanding it to ridicule those in society who are fleeced by the more worldly-wise (III, 562-85).

Works Cited

Abel, Lionel. *Metatheatre. A New View of Dramatic Form.* New York: Hill and Wang, 1963.

Aaróniz, O. *La influencia italiana en el nacimiento de la comedia española.* Madrid, 1969.

Belsey, Catherine. *Critical Practice.* London/New York: Methuen, 1980.

Bentley, Eric. "The *Comedia*: Universality or Uniqueness?" *Hispanic Review* 38 (1970):47-62, and Reichenberger's reply: pp. 163-73.

Burton, Robert. *The Anatomy of Melancholy.* London, 1621.

Calderón de la Barca, Pedro. *El médico de su honra.* Edited by C. A. Jones. Oxford: Clarendon Press, 1961.

—. *La vida es sueño.* Edited by E. W. Hesse. New York: Charles Scribner's Sons, 1961.

Cervantes, Miguel de. *Entremeses.* Edited by J. Canavaggio. Madrid: Taurus, 1981.

Cirlot, J. E. *A Dictionary of Symbols.* Second Edition. Trans. Jack Sage. Intro. by Herbert Read. New York: Philosophical Library, 1971.

Covarrubias Orozco, Sebastián de. *Tesoro de la lengua castellana.* Madrid, 1611.

Crawford, J., P. W. *Spanish Drama before Lope de Vega.* Philadelphia, 1922. Second edition. Bibliographic supplement by Warren T. McCready, 1967.

Culler, Jonathan. *On Deconstruction.* Ithaca: Cornell U P, 1982.

Curry, John V. *Deception in Elizabethan Comedy.* Chicago: Loyola U P, 1955.

Derrida, Jacques. *Of Grammatology.* Trans. Gayatri Chakravorty Spivak. Baltimore/London: The Johns Hopkins U P, 1976.

Gitlitz, David. "How to read a *comedia*: Branching points in the script of Lope's *La discreta enamorada*." *BCom* 40 (Summer, 1988):53-65.

Grismer, Raymond L. *The Influence of Plautus in Spain before Lope de Vega*. New York: Hispanic Institute in the United States, 1944.

Hermenegildo, Alfredo. *Los trágicos españoles del siglo XVI*. Madrid: Fundación Universitaria Española, 1961.

—. *La tragedia en el Renacimiento español*. Barcelona: Planeta, 1973.

Hesse, Everett W. "The Incest Motif in Tirso's *La venganza de Tamar*." *Hispania*, 47 (1964):268-76.

—. "Tirso and the Drama of Imagination and Sexuality." *New Perspectives on "Comedia" Criticism*. Potomac, MD: Studia Humanitatis, 1980. 45-64.

—. "Símbolos sexuales en *El burlador de Sevilla*." *La mujer como víctima en la comedia y otros ensayos*. Barcelona: Puvill, 1987. 52-55.

—. "The *Comedia* as a Theater of the Mind." *The Comedia and Points of View*. Potomac, MD: Scripta Humanistica, 1984. 46-73.

Homer. *The Odyssey*. Translated by Robert Fitzgerald. With drawing by Hans Erm. Garden City, NY: Doubleday, 1961.

Huerta Calvo, Javier. *El teatro medieval y renacentista*. Madrid: Playor, 1984.

Jackson, S. *Melancholia and Depression*. New Haven: Yale U P, 1985.

Jung, C. G. *Two Essays on Analytical Psychology*. Vol. 7 of Collected Works. Princeton: Princeton U P, 1966.

—. *Symbols of Transformation*. Vol. 5 of Collected Works. Princeton: Princeton U P, 1967.

Larue, Gerald. *Sex and the Bible*. Buffalo, NY: Prometheus Books, 1983.

Machiavelli, N. *The Prince*. A bilingual edition. Translated and edited by Mark Musa. New York: St. Martin's Press, 1964.

Marni, Archimede. "Did Tirso employ Counterpassion in his *Burlador de Sevilla*?" *Hispanic Review* 20 (1952):108-22.

Miller, J. Hillis. "The Limits of Pluralism: II The Critic as Host." *Critical Inquiry* 3 (1977):57-77.

Works Cited

Molina, Tirso de. *La venganza de Tamar*. Ed. A. K. G. Paterson. Cambridge: Cambridge U P, 1969. All quotations are from this edition by act and verse number.*

—. *El burlador de Sevilla*. An edition with Introduction, Notes and Glossary by Gerald E. Wade. New York: Scharles Scribner's Sons, 1969.

—. *Don Gil de las calzas verdes*. Ed. de E. W. Hesse y C. L. Moolick. Salamanca: Anaya, 1971.

—. *La venganza de Tamar*. Ed. A. K. G. Paterson. Cambridge: Cambridge U P, 1969.

—. *El vergonzoso en palacio*. Ed. de Francisco Ayala. Madrid: Castalia, 1971.

Morley, S. Griswold. "Color symbolism in Tirso de Molina." *Romanic Review* 8 (1917):77-81.

Murdock, George P. *Social Structure*. New York, 1948.

Norris, Christopher. *Deconstruction: Theory and Practice*. London/New York: Methuen, 1982.

Ovid (Pablius Ovidius Nasi). *Metamorphoses*. Translated by A. D. Melville, with an Introduction and Notes by E. J. Kenney. New York: Oxford U P, 1986.

Pallarés Navarro, Mariano. "Algunos aspectos sexuales en la obra de Tirso de Molina." *Kentucky Romance Quarterly* 19 (1972):3-15.

Parker, A. A. *The Philosophy of Love in Spanish Literature, 1480-1680*. Edited by Terrence O'Reilly for the Edinburgh Press. Edinburgh: Edinburgh U P, 1985.

Ratcliffe, Marjorie. "Matris et munium . . . : Marriage and Law in Medieval Spanish Legislation," *Revista canadiense de estudios hispánicos* 13 (otoño, 1988):94-95.

Reichenberger, A. G. "The Uniqueness of the *comedia*." *Hispanic Review* 27 (1959):303-16.

Saussure, Ferdinand de. *Course in General Linguistics*. Trans. Wade Baskin. London: Fontana, 1974.

---

*While this book was in progress, another edition of the play appeared with the Spanish text on one page and on the facing page the English translation: Tirso de Molina. *Tamar's Revenge. (La venganza de Tamar)*. Translated with an Introduction and Notes by John Lyon. Warminster, England: Aris & Phillips, 1988.

Valencia, Juan O. "La función del símbolo en una comedia de Tirso." *Bulletin of the Comediantes* 26 (Spring, 1974):1-5.

Vega Carpio, Lope de. *El perro del hortelano, El castigo sin venganza*. Ed. A. David Kossof. Clásicos Castalia, 25. Madrid: Castalia, 1971.

—. *Fuenteovejuna. La dama boba*. Ed. de E. W. Hesse. New York: Dell, 1954.

Walker, Barbara G. *The Woman's Encyclopedia of Myths and Secrets*. San Francisco: Harper & Row, 1983.

Warnock, Mary. *Imagination*. London: Faber & Faber, 1976.

Index to the Books Published by E. W. Hesse

Calderón. New York: Twayne, 1967.

Contents

1. The Age of Calderón 13
2. The *Comedia* 19
3. The Spanish Theater of the Golden Age 32
4. Facets of Calderón's Dramatic and Poetic Art 37
5. The Cloak-and-Sword Plays 48
6. The Costumbristic Plays 57
7. Religious Dramas 64
8. The Historical Plays 94
9. The Honor Tragedies 104
10. The Mythological Plays 123
11. The Philosophical Plays 137
12. Calderón's Minor Theater 149
13. Calderón and the Critics 156

Análisis e Interpretación de la Comedia. Madrid: Castalia, 1968.

Contenido

Prólogo 11

1. Lope de Vega
   El caballero de Olmedo 21
   El villano en su rincón 30

2. Tirso de Molina
   Don gil de las calzas verdes............43
   La venganza de Tamar............51
3. Calderón de la Barca
   Eco y Narciso............69
   La vida es sueño............84

La Comedia y sus Intérpretes. Madrid: Castalia, 1972.

Contenido

Capítulo Primero.	Introducción............	17
Capítulo Segundo.	La Trama............	25
Capítulo Tercero.	Personajes y caracterización............	31
Capítulo Cuarto.	La comedia y la estilística............	57
Capítulo Quinto.	La comedia como tragedia............	81
Capítulo Sexto.	La comedia como obra cómica............	99
Capítulo Séptimo.	La comedia y su interpretacíon............	125
Capítulo Octavo.	La comedia y el tema............	145
Capítulo Noveno.	La comedia y los problemas sociales............	181

Interpretando la Comedia. Madrid: Porrúa Turanzas, 1977.

Índice

Primera Parte: Lope de Vega
I. La perversión del amor en *El castigo sin venganza*............5
II. El arte de encubrir la realidad en *El castigo sin venganza*............19
III. Las nociones de amor en *Fuenteovejuna*............31

Segunda Parte: Tirso de Molina
IV. La imaginación creadora en *El vergonzoso en palacio*............55

Tercera Parte: Calderón
V. La personalidad de Gutierre en *El médico de su honra*............71

VI. Los tribunales del honor en *El médico de su honra* 83
VII. La realidad psíquica en *La vida es sueño* 99
VIII. El arte de metateatro en *La vida es sueño* 115

                Cuarta Parte: Aspectos de la comedia
IX. El doble criterio de valores en la comedia 131
X. Perspectivas sobre la tragedia en el Siglo de Oro..................................153

New Perspectives on Comedia Criticism. Madrid: Porrúa Turanzas, 1980.

                            Contenido

1. The *Comedia* and its Man-Woman Relationships..1
2. Tirso and the Drama of Imagination and Sexuality 45
3. A Psychological Approach to *El médico de su honra* 65
4. *La vida es sueño* and its Vision of a Socio-Moral Psychology................... 84
5. The Nature of Justice and the Psychic Causes of Injustice
   in the *Comedia* 103
6. Epilogue 144

Essays on Spanish Letters of the Golden Age. Madrid: Porrúa-Turanzas, 1981.

                            Contents

                  The Picaresque Narrative
Lazarillo de Tormes and the Playing of a Role 1
Lazarillo de Termes and the Way of the World 19
The Protean Changes in Quevedo's *Buscón*.. 36

                      The *Comedia*
The Role of the Mind in Lope's *El caballero de Olmedo*................................. 57
The Sense of Lope's *El villano en su rincón* 68
The Gender-Identity Issue in Tirso's *El Aquiles*... 84
The Publication of Calderón's Plays in the Seventeenth Century................... 98

Calderón and Velázquez..117
The Alienation Problem in Calderón's *La Devoción de la Cruz*.....................136
Calderón's *El monstruo de los jardines* and its Sexual Problem....................156
Honor and Behavioral Patterns in *El médico de su honra*............................169
La vida es sueño and the Paradox of Violence..203

Theology, Sex and the Comedia. Madrid: Porrúa, Turanzas, 1982.

Contents

1. Theology, sex and the *Comedia*..1
2. Calderón's *El mágico prodigioso* and the role of the devil.......................38
3. Calderón's *Eco y Narciso* and the split personality..................................53
4. Tirso's Don Juan and the opposing self...62
5. *La vida es sueño* and the labyrinth of illusion..70
6. The creative imagination in Lope de Vega's theater..................................80
7. Calderón's Semíramis: A personality profile...95
8. *La vida es sueño* and the divided self..112

The Comedia and Points of View. Potomoc, MD: Scripta Humanistica, 1984.

Contents

1. *La vida es sueño* and contemporary criticism...1
2. The *comedia* and psychology..14
3. The sociology of Lope's *El villano en su rincón*......................................34
4. The *comedia* as a theater of the mind..46
5. A socio-political approach to *Fuenteovejuna*..74
6. Ironic dimensions in Tirso's theater..85
7. Varities of the mother archetype and role playing in the *comedia*........103
8. The hermaphrodite archetype and maternal symbols in the *comedia*....125
9. Fear and courage as psycho-literary motifs in the *comedia*...................146

La mujer como víctima en la comedia y otros ensayos. Barcelona: Puvill, 1987.

Contenido

Capítulo Primero.	La mujer como víctima en la comedia............................. 17
Capítulo Segundo.	Simbolismo sexual en *El burlador de Sevilla* 45
Capítulo Tercero.	La visión del 'yo' en el contexto social del *Burlador de Sevilla* 67
Capítulo Cuarto.	La Semíramis de Calderón: mito de la mujer fálica........ 85
Capítulo Quinto.	La interacción del pensar y sentir en *El vergonzoso de palacio*.. 97
Capítulo Sexto.	Variaciones sobre el tema del amor en la comedia........117

The Comedia and Human Relationships. Barcelona: Puvill, 1989.

Contents

Prologue...7
Act One: Man's Inhumanity to Woman.. 11
Act Two: Woman's Inhumanity to Man 29
Act Three: The Ethics of Love and Friendship in Ruiz de Alarcón's
   El examen de maridos.. 45
Act Four: (Mis)reading Dramatic Signs in Tirso's *El vergonzoso
   en palacio*.. 61
Act Five: Reason and the Passions in Calderón's *La cisma
   de Inglaterra*... 77
Epilogue 95